Tributes to

John Hope Franklin

Tributes to
John Hope Franklin
Scholar, Mentor, Father, Friend

EDITED BY

Beverly Jarrett

UNIVERSITY OF MISSOURI PRESS
COLUMBIA AND LONDON

Library of Congress Cataloging-in-Publication Data

Tributes to John Hope Franklin : scholar, mentor, father,
friend / edited by Beverly Jarrett.
     p. cm.
Includes bibliographical references and index.
    ISBN 0-8262-1504-1 (alk. paper)
    1. Franklin, John Hope, 1915– 2. Franklin, John
Hope, 1915– —Political and social views. 3. African American
historians—Biography. 4. Historians—United States—
Biography. 5. African Americans—Historiography.
6. United States—Race relations—Historiography.
I. Jarrett, Beverley, 1940– II. Franklin, John Hope, 1915–
E175.5.F73 T75 2004
305.896'073'0092—dc22

                                 2003017515

Designer: Kristie Lee
Typesetter: Crane Composition, Inc.
Printer and binder: Thomson-Shore, Inc.
Typefaces: Minion and Shelly Volante

Contents

Preface

BEVERLY JARRETT

ISTORIAN Wilma King must be credited with the idea for this book. It was she who planned the session at the 2002 meeting of the Organization of American Historians (OAH) at which many of these tributes to John Hope Franklin were delivered. She knew of my own deep affection for the subject of her session and thus saw to it that I was among the vast crowd that assembled for the occasion. As I listened to the very different recountings of the vital contributions John Hope Franklin has made to the lives of many distinguished scholars, I knew I was listening to a book—a book I was determined to publish.

Alfred A. Moss Jr., Genna Rae McNeil, George M. Fredrickson, John W. "Whit" Franklin, Loren Schweninger, and Mary Frances Berry all spoke so poignantly of this giant—as teacher, as colleague, as father, as friend. It was immediately clear to me that what they'd said needed to be preserved.

Once word spread that the University of Missouri Press would be publishing this collection of tributes to our common hero, Catherine Clinton sent me a copy of some earlier, briefer words of praise by equally distinguished scholars. Those earlier tributes had been published in 1997, on the fiftieth anniversary of the publication of Franklin's *From Slavery to Freedom,* by the *Journal of Blacks in Higher Education.* That journal very generously allowed us to include those pieces in this book.

Soon thereafter, I heard from Walter B. Hill Jr. about another celebration of our subject—this one at the eighty-seventh conference of the Association for the Study of African American Life and History (ASALH). We secured those other tributes for inclusion in our book, pieces by four respected scholars: Robert L. Harris Jr., Darlene Clark Hine, Walter B. Hill Jr., and Daryl Michael Scott. And finally we persuaded David Levering Lewis to allow us to include the tribute he delivered at Duke University on the occasion of Franklin's eightieth birthday.

Tributes to John Hope Franklin: Scholar, Mentor, Father, Friend needs no justification. Its subject justifies its publication. America is filled with citizens, both inside and outside academia, who recognize and appreciate John Hope Franklin. Most know something of Franklin's powerful efforts to improve our lives. How many doors he has opened for others can never be accurately measured, but these varied tributes to him demonstrate some of the countless ways in which he has led us all toward continuing the struggle for realization of the American dream of equality and freedom.

As the celebratory event at the 2002 OAH meeting came to its close, Dr. Franklin was asked for a brief response. A somewhat frail, almost enfeebled gentleman walked slowly and deliberately from the audience to the stage. Announcing at once that he was again "breaking the rules" (this time those laid down for him by his physicians), Franklin addressed the crowd. He'd been told not to make any more speeches or accept any more honorary degrees, but to guard his health and save his strength. Nonetheless, Franklin responded poignantly to these tributes. Standing tall and speaking with his usual strength and wisdom, he thanked the panelists, expressing himself with predictable modesty, and urging us all to go forward in the good fight.

I couldn't help remembering the first time I'd seen this extraordinary human, in 1976, when I served as copyeditor for *A Southern Odyssey: Travelers in the Antebellum North.* As I recalled our other shared book endeavors, I also remembered many special times in our thirty-year friendship.

My readings of these diverse tributes to John Hope Franklin, some with very touching and personal memories or stories, led me to conclude that it might not be improper to include one of my own rather personal memories of watching the master work. I can't recall the precise year, but this experience occurred sometime in the 1980s, a time when it was not yet ordinary to see a black man and a white woman alone together—at least not in the Deep South.

John Hope, as I always call him, was doing some research in Baton Rouge. We had several good visits during that week—sharing meals and sharing cooking adventures (he's an outstanding cook). But the experience I want to relate happened during a fishing trip to a camp near St. Francisville, Louisiana, that was owned by an acquaintance of mine.

We set out on that little journey one morning—just the two of us—and I promptly got lost. I believe we got some directions from a black policeman, whose face showed a bit of wonder at this white lady with a southern accent driving this black gentleman and asking for directions to a turnoff toward the uninhabited woods.

Finally we found the turnoff and located the fishing pond. No sooner had we got out of the car and begun to gather our fishing poles and tackle box than we heard a slow-moving, decrepit pickup truck heading in our direction. The fellow who got out of the truck and shuffled toward us had come to see just who we were and what we were doing there. (The owner of the property had not warned me that he paid a local to "keep an eye on the place" for him.) My first thought was that we'd encountered real trouble. Would my friend John Hope be spoken to unkindly? Would we both be run off the place? Would John Hope be ill-treated and I unable to prevent such mistreatment? I've often thought since then that my fears that morning were fears quite common to the experience of a black American.

After I told the man we'd been given permission to fish by the owner of the place, John Hope took charge of the exchange. He gently altered the spirit of our conversation by asking the man about fish—what kind we'd be likely to find, what size they'd be, what sort of bait they'd prefer. Before it was over, the man had told us the best side of the pond to fish, where to go to buy better bait, what kind to ask for. He ultimately led us to a nearby bait shack and bid us farewell and good fishing.

Of course one ending of this fishing tale is the ongoing argument John Hope and I have had over who caught the most fish and who caught the biggest one. But the other, less debatable and more instructive ending to the story—one I've contemplated for twenty years now—is how masterfully this learned man spoke to this stranger in language both of them understood. Without a moment's hesitation, he dismantled the property guard's uncertainty about us, won the man over to our side, and enlisted his aid in whatever success we had fishing.

All who have known John Hope Franklin have stories like this one, which I regard as a hands-on example of the lessons he's been teaching us throughout his life. Practicing what he preaches, he brings out the best in any person and in any circumstances. As I watched John Hope speak to those assembled to honor him, I recalled many such moments from my long friendship with the subject of this book, including a less immediately personal but equally powerful memory, that of his visit to the University of Missouri in 1992.

It was at the University of Missouri that he delivered the lectures that became *The Color Line: Legacy for the Twenty-First Century.* In that book he had given us all the same challenge that this frailer but no less determined man gave the audience assembled to honor him in 2002. Since his remarks that evening were spontaneous, it may be reasonable to quote here the more formal expression of Franklin's lifelong challenge to his fellow Americans:

> Perhaps the very first thing we need to do as a nation and as individual members of a society is to confront our past and

see it for what it is. It is a past that is filled with some of the ugliest possible examples of racial brutality and degradation in human history. We need to recognize it for what it was and is and not explain it away, excuse it, or justify it. Having done that, we should then make a good-faith effort to turn our history around so that we can see it in front of us, so that we can avoid doing what we have done for so long. If we do that, whites will discover that African Americans possess the same human qualities that other Americans possess, and African Americans will discover that white Americans are capable of the most sublime expressions of human conduct of which all human beings are capable. Then, we need to do everything possible to emphasize the positive qualities that all of us have, qualities which we have never utilized to the fullest, but which we must utilize if we are going to solve the problem of the color line in the twenty-first century.

How someone could deliver the same message for more than half a century without ever seeming to repeat himself is surely a wonder. But that is what John Hope Franklin—the historian's historian and the American's American—has done. And that is why, or at least part of why, he is the subject of these uniquely varied tributes to him, to his work, to his message. Without him we would not have advanced nearly so far. With him, may we all go farther still.

Tributes to
John Hope Franklin

Introductory Remarks

MARY FRANCES BERRY

IRST I MUST say that I am somewhat biased on the subject of John Hope Franklin. I greatly admire him as a scholar, and he has always been a role model for me. I happen to believe that every one of his publications constitutes a major historical contribution. But it is *The Militant South,* too seldom praised, that remains the best work ever done on southern culture and violence associated with honor.

I love and respect John Hope Franklin all the more because he cared enough to dedicate a book to me. Imagine my surprise when on Christmas Day 1992 a special-delivery package arrived at my house; I opened it to discover a copy of John Hope's *The Color Line: Legacy for the Twenty-First Century,* with a wonderful note saying, "The dedication page shows that 'I wish you a merry Christmas.'" When I turned to the dedication page I saw, "To Mary Frances Berry, Courageous Fighter Against the Color Line."

Franklin's world renown as a historian and his consistent advocacy for the importance of the teaching of history are reason enough to give him praise. But I stand in awe also of his major contributions to the formulation of public policy designed to help our nation achieve the goal of equal opportunity for all. Of course, his name adorns the most important race relations legal briefs. Wherever I travel I go in his wake, since he has been there before, invited to lecture to audiences of students, scholars, and laypersons in every part of the world. In addition, he has helped to select diplomats to represent the United States abroad. His leadership of President Clinton's race initiative, One America, through some very choppy waters, alone merits the highest accolades.

John Hope Franklin has offered consistent encouragement as I, and other historians, have muddled through endless research on various projects, always ready to let us know when it is time for the writing to begin. If he hadn't told me that when I was in the midst of what would become *The Pig Farmer's Daughter and Other Tales of Law and Justice,* I would still be muddling. He has shown by example that historical writing can be done with felicity and grace, without sacrificing the attention to method and objectivity that careful scholarship requires.

His graduate students and the legions of scholars who attempt to follow in his footsteps carry on the Franklin legacy. I admire all of his many books and articles, but *From Slavery to Freedom* undoubtedly has had a major impact on the teaching of American history. This book has established itself as the preeminent synthesis of the history of African Americans. Equally significant, it has become a model for how a member of an immigrant group of color can write about the group's experience in ways acceptable to the group and consistent with the highest standards of historians at large.

It is altogether fitting and proper that we should honor John Hope Franklin for making the study and teaching of American history more inclusive and more whole. Still publishing and producing at the height of his intellectual powers, John Hope Franklin—friend, mentor, and role model—is indeed exceedingly worthy to be praised.

Race, History,
and John Hope Franklin
DAVID LEVERING LEWIS

THESE WORDS are to pay tribute to a pioneer scholar; a splendid humanist; a shining model to generations of students, scholars, and activists; and, to those who've had the privilege and pleasure of knowing him personally, a man of prodigious generosity, prudent counsel, and unaffected grace. John Hope Franklin's qualities have been described by his friend Vann Woodward, in *Thinking Back: The Perils of Writing History,* as "perfect intellectual and moral poise with inexhaustible good humor." A feast of John Hope Franklin's essays and addresses, entitled *Race and History: Selected Essays,* appeared from a major university press a few years ago. One of the addresses included in that volume makes the large challenge of appreciating his illustrious career much easier. In that address, entitled "John Hope Franklin: A Life of Learning" and delivered before the American Council of Learned Societies in April 1988, Franklin recalls the ninetieth-birthday wisdom of the immortal composer of ragtime, Eubie Blake. "If I had known that I would live this long," said Blake, "I would have taken better care of myself."

3

Well, John Hope must have intuited that his would be a longevity resembling that of another Fisk graduate and scholar, W. E. B. Du Bois, about whom he wrote so sagaciously in his compact book *The Color Line: Legacy for the Twenty-First Century,* because he has taken very good care indeed of himself over his more than eighty years. More important, by doing so, he has also been able to take great, good care of a broad swath of American political and social history.

A truth that our amnesiac and racially correct era needs to share about Franklin's life—one that cannot be overemphasized for the cautionary and exemplary lessons it contains—is that, in that time long ago, before he become John Hope Franklin, author of *From Slavery to Freedom* (the book that virtually created the industry of African American studies, now in its bestselling eighth edition), as well as ten other monographs; or John Hope Franklin, the first person of African descent to chair academic departments in historically white institutions (first, Brooklyn College in 1956 and then the University of Chicago in 1967); or John Hope Franklin, first person of African and probably non-WASP descent to be elected president of the United Chapters of Phi Beta Kappa (1973–1976) and to achieve the further distinction of holding the presidencies of the Southern Historical Association (1969–1970), the Organization of American Historians (1974–1975), and the American Historical Association (1978–1979); or John Hope Franklin, holder, if I'm not mistaken, according to the *Guinness Book of Records,* of the most honorary degrees awarded to anybody; and John Hope Franklin, cultivator of orchids of incomparable beauty—what we must not forget in the glow of celebration is the truth that, long before there was John Hope Franklin the Institution, there was John Hope Franklin the Rentiesville, Oklahoma, kid born in a place where, and growing to adolescence in a time when, failing to take extremely good care of oneself could be fatal.

Even though John Hope was blessed with caring parents and the modest advantages of his father's law practice, life in early-twentieth-century Oklahoma was no crystal stair. Look at what he wrote about his early years: "The quality of life in Rentiesville was low as one can imagine. There was no electricity, running water, or inside plumbing. There was no entertainment or diversion of any kind—no parks, playgrounds, libraries, or newspapers. . . . Now and then one went to Checotah, six miles away, to shop. That was not always pleasant, such as the time when my mother, sister, and I were ejected from the train because my mother refused to move from the coach designated for whites."[1] How many Rosa Parks there must have been before the last Rosa Parks refused to be Jim Crowed in Montgomery! Then, just as the Franklin family prepared to move in 1921 from Rentiesville to Tulsa with its thriving black business community, the Tulsa community was destroyed by a race riot. Franklin is now writing a personal account (based in part on his father's autobiography, *My Life and an Era: The Autobiography of Buck Colbert Franklin*) of those fast-fading, separate-but-very-unequal times that younger students such as Carl Ditmer and Neil McMillen have reconstructed from a greater distance. The first installment of his work, "Vintage Years: The First Decade," enlivened the audience at the 1994 Thirty-First Cosmos Club Award.

At Fisk University, where Franklin matriculated in 1931 at the age of sixteen, he only wanted to prepare himself for law school, and so he arrived there intending to rack up good grades and get on. But he did not always get those good grades, it seems, partly because of the quality of the segregated Tulsa high school preparation, but mainly because he had to work three jobs in order to stay in college. One mediocre grade he got pushed him over the edge—C-Plus in Contemporary Civilization. It rankles him still, for he wrote: "If there was anyone to listen to my case today I would insist that my examinations be reevaluated and my grade raised accordingly!" A Fisk classmate—an English major—lent a consoling ear to these plaints for fifty years, but she, he says, could "afford to be charitable," for

1. "John Hope Franklin: A Life of Learning," in *Race and History: Selected Essays, 1938–1988* (Baton Rouge: Louisiana State University Press, 1989), 278.

Mrs. Aurelia Whittingham Franklin earned a B-Plus in Contemporary Civilization.[2] The future Mrs. Franklin, who was born in Goldsboro, was John Hope's rock in the somewhat treacherous waters of Fisk. By chance, my wife recently read the pleasant piece written by Franklin for a booklet about his romance and marriage—"For Better, for Worse," he calls it—in which Aurelia Whittingham is described as having informed him in no uncertain terms that he was not to yield to the dean who urged him to step aside as Student Council president in favor of another candidate. "Her outrage was controlled but quite obvious," he wrote. Fisk was something of an oasis in the Jim Crow South, a place of relative privilege. But Franklin and most of his classmates seldom went into downtown Nashville. And on one ghastly evening, white hoodlums from Nashville charged into the Fisk neighborhood, seized a young man, and dragged him away to be lynched. As president of the student body, Franklin protested to the mayor, the governor, and even, to no avail, to President Franklin Roosevelt when he visited the campus.

Like so many gifted actors in search of a script, John Hope came to his vocation by chance. A Yankee professor from Maine, Theodore Shirley Currier, a legendary character at Fisk, turned him on to history. Twenty years later, Currier had that same charismatic impact on another student who, like John Hope, intended to coast through college on the way to law school. I speak of myself, and in doing so I beg the reader's indulgence of a sidebar description I wrote elsewhere of Currier, this professor to whom both Franklin and I have dedicated monographs. He was a handsome, well-built, short man who chain smoked as he walked quickly back and forth, alternately stabbing the air for emphasis or manipulating a cigarette like a baton as he lectured in a nasal New England brogue. Ted Currier was the last of the best of the Mr. Chips breed—a spellbinding lecturer with total-recall memory and a quicksilver mind that made it possible (if not pedagogically legitimate) for him to teach

2. Ibid., 281.

courses in Latin American and Russian history, as well as American, with apparently equal competence. One of the youngest students ever admitted to Harvard's graduate history department, Currier had been at Fisk since he was twenty-two. When I knew him, he was probably in his late fifties. His bachelor abode on the campus was an after-hours' classroom and tavern enveloped in smoke and throbbing with sessions about every conceivable historical topic and most everything else. Currier was fiercely proud of one of his majors: a Harvard Ph.D. named John Hope Franklin.

Currier became Franklin's mentor and lifetime friend, and when Franklin came up short of tuition money for Harvard's graduate school, he stood guarantor of the $500 bank loan he arranged. Franklin earned the Master's in nine months flat under Arthur Schlesinger Sr., but he was not at first entirely happy with the dissertation topic he eventually chose. The original proposal was for a topic having nothing to do with what was then known as Negro history. But Franklin experienced at Harvard—albeit mildly and certainly fortuitously—that marginalizing of intellectual options available to scholars of color about which he has written so compellingly in his famous essay "The Dilemma of the American Negro Scholar" (1963). Fifteen years after Charles Harris Wesley, his Harvard predecessor, had been dissuaded by his adviser from writing a history of the defeat of the Confederacy, typecasting still reigned. "This was a tragedy," Franklin asserted. "Negro scholarship had foundered on the rocks of racism. It had been devoured by principles of separatism, of segregation. It had become the victim of the view that there was some 'mystique' about Negro studies, similar to the view that there was some "mystique" about Negro spirituals which required that a person possess a black skin in order to sing them. This was not scholarship; it was folklore, it was voodoo."[3]

How strange it was to see the meaning of these words stood on their head in Vann Woodward's famous review-essay of Dinesh

---

3. "The Dilemma of the American Negro Scholar," in ibid., 301.

D'Souza's *Illiberal Education* in the *New York Review of Books* for December 1990! But let's be clear about the point here: it was surely not the case that Franklin believed that African American history was not worth doing back in 1936; rather, it was that those in the profession who thought little of it wanted him and his contemporaries to be confined to it. As I read the first essay to be published in a scholarly journal by a twenty-three-year-old John Hope Franklin—"Edward Bellamy and the Nationalist Movement"—appearing in the December 1938 *New England Quarterly*—I contemplated this most striking example of the Negro scholar's "dilemma." Based on the personal papers of Bellamy, the cooperation of his widow, and broad reading, this felicitously written venture demonstrated early on a scope of learning, ease of synthesis, and aptitude for biography that would come to maturity in later years in a rich profile of Reconstruction congressman John R. Lynch and the long-awaited biography of George Washington Williams.

I would ask John Hope if it must not have been at Harvard that he embraced a conviction about his craft, eloquently stated in his 1988 address to the American Council of Learned Societies: "Many years ago, when I was a fledgling historian, I decided that one way to make certain that the learning process would continue was to write different kinds of history, even as one remained in the same field." By the time he had finished his Ph.D. course work in the spring of 1939, he had mastered the cutting-edge scholarship of the day and experienced intimately at Harvard another manifestation of American scapegoating. As a member of the Henry Adams Club, he proposed for club president an acquaintance he thought was the most active and brightest of the graduate history students. He was told, however, that, "although he did not have some of the more reprehensible Jewish traits, he was still a Jew." He lost much of his respect for dear old Harvard after that.[4]

To complete the research for his doctoral dissertation, published

---

4. "A Life of Learning," in ibid., 290, 284.

as *The Free Negro in North Carolina* (1943), and for such classics as *The Militant South, 1800–1861* (1956) and *Reconstruction after the Civil War* (1961), Franklin boldly went where few African American scholars had gone before. He presented himself to often red-faced custodians of archival collections in such places as Raleigh, North Carolina, and Montgomery, Alabama. The State Archivist at Raleigh in the summer of 1939 had never anticipated the petition of a young black scholar for access to his records. A Yale history Ph.D., he condescended to make special arrangements for a Harvard ABD. Returning after a few days as he had been instructed, Franklin was escorted to a "small room outfitted with a table and chair which was to be my private office for the next four years."[5] Was it not Tallulah Bankhead's sister-in-law who imperiously commanded that research facilities be made available to Franklin in Montgomery? When we recall that a major criticism leveled against Du Bois's *Black Reconstruction in America* by professional historians was that he failed to work the archives, we might be less caustic in light of Franklin's research experiences. It is hard to imagine Du Bois motoring from "white" courthouse to university library entreating entry of rude custodians or even, should he have been admitted, agreeing to remain out of sight in small, windowless back rooms poring over tax rolls and property ledgers.

John Hope Franklin's perseverance was to pay off for his profession in a spectacular manner. *The Free Negro in North Carolina* descended along a historiographical line from Carter Woodson and John Russell through James M. Wright, but, in contrast to such useful and earnest antecedents as Woodson's *Free Negro Heads of Families in the United States in 1830* (1925) and Wright's *The Free Negro in Maryland* (1921), his monograph, along with Luther P. Jackson's contemporary study of Virginia, was distinctly modern in analytical robustness and research archaeology. It placed North Carolina's slaves without masters in a social context with defined economic

5. Ibid., 288.

underpinnings. It disclosed the delicate tensions and ambiguous ties of this class of people to their white analogues and superiors. Although set in a later time frame and exploring political combinations impossible before Reconstruction, Helen Edmond's pioneering monograph, *The Negro and Fusion Politics in North Carolina* (1951), and Frenise Logan's *The Negro in North Carolina, 1876–1894* (1964) clearly owed much to the electric charge imparted by Franklin's book to the field of African American state studies.

From Slavery to Freedom: A History of Negro Americans (1947), his next book, would become the benchmark for a field that had waited a quarter-century since Woodson's serviceable but flawed work, *The Negro in Our History* (1922), for a synoptic treatment. One senses a certain professional caginess in its preface, as Alfred A. Knopf released this most revisionist of general histories. "I have attempted to avoid a subjective and unscientific treatment of the subject," Franklin stated. Written accessibly in order to reach a wide audience, *From Slavery to Freedom* traversed four hundred years from the African background to the era of the G.I. Bill, presenting the antebellum struggles of the so-called free Negro and the politics of Reconstruction in a manner altogether startling to a public weaned on Ulrich B. Phillips and Claude Bowers. In our own revisionist era in which paradigms rise and fall almost like the hemlines on Paris fashions, it should be recalled, as Peter Novick's *That Noble Dream* tells us, that the history profession of the 1940s deferred to a mythos of objectivity. Insofar as people of color and women were concerned, objectivity meant that any historian who challenged the professional consensus by investing these populations with agency risked censure as a propagandist undeserving of the respect of colleagues. Franklin's risk would pay off.

But his next offering was in a sense more professionally audacious. Not only did it run against the grain of the regnant Neoconservative School, represented outstandingly by Daniel Boorstin and Louis Hartz, which claimed for America a unique society characterized by a consensus upon a homogeneous tradition of thought—

that of Lockean liberalism—but it also owed nothing to the earlier economic reductionism of Charles A. Beard and Vernon Louis Parrington and other progressive historians. *The Militant South, 1800–1861* (1956) was among the earliest works heralding an interpretive shift to a political-cultural paradigm in which economic and political forces are focused through the lens of hegemonic belief systems. Taking Wilbur Cash's apothegm that the antebellum white man "did not think, he felt," Franklin elevated the South's pandemic violence into the organizing principle of its society. "In the South," his preface maintains, "militant race superiority evolved out of the defense of plantation slavery, to become an ingredient in the culture."

Staples of the profession such as Genovese's *The Political Economy of Slavery* (1965) and (as acknowledged in its sources) Bertram Wyatt-Brown's *Honor and Violence in the Old South* (1986) unmistakably derive from the analytical spirit of this seminal work. Standard preoccupations such as the tariff, states' rights abstractions, and sectional rivalry as causes of the Civil War were given minimal play in order to recover the lost insight that the South's peculiar institution had locked it into a peculiar culture in which commerce, profit motive, and indeed Lockean liberalism were repeatedly short-circuited. Chapter 7—"A Little Learning"—is an enduring gem. To be sure, Franklin stresses that monocausal explanations are deficient. Violence and the martial spirit did not cause the War between the States, he stresses. "But this tradition, together with the preparations to support and nourish it, gave the South a self-confidence that strengthened its determination to take the fatal step of secession."[6] Not since Du Bois's coruscant chapter on the plantocracy in *Black Reconstruction* had an African American scholar mounted such a cogent indictment. A detail of more than incidental relevance is that *The Militant South* barely escaped rejection on the way to its

---

6. *The Militant South, 1800–1861* (Cambridge: Harvard University Press, 1956).

Harvard University Press publication when one distinguished outside reader questioned why an African American's views on the subject should be of any interest.

Mention of Du Bois brings us to *Reconstruction after the Civil War* (1961), Franklin's chef d'oeuvre, and to another personal sidebar. This one is my vivid recollection of our departed colleague Nathan Huggins's rather annoyed reaction to Franklin's 1979 presidential address to the American Historical Association. In this address, entitled "Mirror for Americans: A Century of Reconstruction History," Franklin observed that "recent scholarship on the Reconstruction era leaves the impression that we may be reaching the point, after a century of effort, . . . when we no longer need to shape Reconstruction history to suit our own current needs."[7] Yet, because he omitted any mention of his own book on the subject, Huggins thought he had been much too modest. Huggins, like I, would have been more happy if the address had left less to the vagaries of the collective memory even of historians. The curious omission of *Reconstruction after the Civil War* from the bibliography of what is now the standard work on the subject shows that Huggins fretted with good reason. Yet, if, as I fear, Franklin's Reconstruction book may have been somewhat underappreciated, there is a flattering paradox here, as Eric Anderson and Alfred Moss observed in the collection of essays in Franklin's honor, *The Facts of Reconstruction* (1991): "When a scholar helps to discredit a previous understanding—if the job is done thoroughly enough—he often is rewarded in an odd way." Anderson and Moss continue, "subsequent researchers may accept his insights as obvious."[8]

Once again, Franklin followed in the steps of Du Bois, that flinty iconoclast who has served as role model. In December 1909, before an AHA audience that included William Dunning himself, Du Bois

7. "Mirror for Americans: A Century of Reconstruction History," in *Race and History,* 397–98.

8. Eric Anderson and Alfred A. Moss, Jr., eds., *The Facts of Reconstruction: Essays in Honor of John Hope Franklin* (Baton Rouge: Louisiana State University Press, 1991), ix.

read the paper "Reconstruction and Its Benefits" to momentary applause followed by indefinite relegation. Du Bois contended that Reconstruction had been neither an unwise experiment nor an unmediated disaster for the South and concluded by stating: "Practically the whole new growth of the South has been accomplished under the laws which black men helped to frame thirty years ago. I know of no greater compliment to Negro suffrage."[9] When Du Bois returned to the charge in 1935 with the publication of *Black Reconstruction in America,* the official response of the historical profession ranged from silence in the *American Historical Review* to disdain in the seminars of the academy. But the book's influence gradually surfaced in the writings of William Hesseltine, Howard K. Beale, and a handful of other white historians. There was also, to be sure, a parallel modification in Dunningite orthodoxy nudged along by the work of southerners Francis Simkins and Robert Woody on South Carolina and the much later Mississippi monograph by Vernon Wharton. African American historian and Hesseltine student Benjamin Quarles incorporated much Reconstruction revisionism in his 1948 biography of Frederick Douglass, as did Howard University historian Rayford W. Logan in *The Negro in American Life and Thought: The Nadir, 1877–1901* (1954).

The dress rehearsal for Franklin's eventual capital role in these debates was the review of Merton Coulter's Dunningite last hurrah— *The South during Reconstruction, 1865–1877* (1947)—which famously asserted: "There can be no sensible departure from the well-known facts of the Reconstruction program as it was applied to the South."[10] In the fall 1948 issue of the *Journal of Negro Education,* Franklin's "Whither Reconstruction Historiography?" went well beyond Beale's eight-year-old *AHR* essay in rebutting Coulter's "well-known facts." The gauntlet had been thrown, and the battle was definitively joined

9. Du Bois, "Reconstruction and Its Benefits," *American Historical Review* (July 1910), reprinted in *Writings by W. E. B. Du Bois in Periodicals Edited by Others,* ed. Herbert Aptheker (Millwood, N.Y.: Kraus-Thomson Organization, 1982), 2:6–22 (quote on 22).

10. E. Merton Coulter, *The South during Reconstruction, 1865–1877* (Baton Rouge: Louisiana State University Press, 1947).

on behalf of the African American's historic role with the publica-tion of Franklin's 1961 book. *Reconstruction after the Civil War* not only walloped the Dunningites, but it also undertook to generalize about the era. Franklin filled in Du Bois's claim that corruption was nationwide, that "black rule" was mostly historical agitprop, and that some positive accomplishments obtained in education and prison reform. The book also returned to the role of southern white vio-lence in the overthrow of Reconstruction—not merely as an epi-sodic and limited factor but as one that was indispensable. Four years after the publication of Franklin's Reconstruction monograph, Kenneth Stampp's revisionist general history and Joel Williamson's germinal *After Slavery: The Negro in South Carolina during Recon-struction, 1861–1877* would appear.

Let us fast-forward now through the innumerable distinctions ranging from UNESCO delegate to Jefferson Lecturer in the Hu-manities to William Pitt Professor of American History at Cam-bridge, to election to the Oklahoma Hall of Fame and the award of the Encyclopedia Britannica's Gold Medal for Dissemina-tion of Knowledge, onward to the Charles Frankel Prize of the National En-dowment for the Humanities at the hands of President Clinton—and in 1995 (in a New York occasion I was privileged to share with him) to the Bruce Catton Prize for Distinguished Service presented by the Society of American Historians. Teaching has always been as important in Franklin's career as the research and writing of his nu-merous books. He taught many of our best and brightest African American students at St. Augustine College, at the North Carolina Central University in Durham, and at Howard University before as-suming the history chairmanship at Brooklyn College in 1956. That appointment resulted in a front-page story in the *New York Times.* My assumption is that if a similar appointment today would go un-remarked on page 1, this would be evidence of racial progress rather than of public indifference to the esteem in which some historians hold other historians. Franklin's tenure as chair at the University of Chicago (1967–1970) was a period of exceptional recruitment and productivity for the history department. His second career at Duke has been a living invalidation of the concept of retirement. I think, naturally enough, of the nonagenarian subject of my biography. Du Bois was fond of saying that he would have been acclaimed had he died at fifty, but that at seventy-five his death was practically requested. When John Hope reached the age of eighty, universities were still requesting his vita.

But he has another achievement—in addition to writing and teaching—one that has, I believe, the very highest exemplary meaning for all of us, irrespective of race or age, but of particular value to young men and women who, although they may applaud his professional attainments and pay formal respect to the life of the mind, do not really appreciate the value of what he has done as a scholar in the so-called real world. They should know—we all should—that John Hope is that rarest of historians who places his knowledge in the service of social progress. Published in 1974, the talk given as "The Historian and Public Policy" is a wonderful read. I would urge the widest dissemination of this pamphlet in the academy, in law schools, among the general public, and indeed to anyone interested in the praxis of history. Franklin distinguishes there between two versions of scholarly intervention into public policy. One is of the partisan and defensive character of, say, a Claude Bowers writing in service to the Democratic Party on Jefferson and Hamilton, or of an Ulrich B. Phillips shoring up slavery. The other intervention is, he writes, "more interested in *how* historical events can provide some basis for desirable change."[11] He goes on to cite a famous 1908 case in which Louis Brandeis argued successfully before the Supreme Court for a maximum on working hours for women in a brief that delved into female characteristics, woman's historic role, and matters of physique.

Since then, the court has sometimes been willing to admit historical as well as sociological evidence, Franklin says. In 1953, he shared

11. "The Historian and the Public Policy," in *Race and History,* 311.

with others an opportunity to play Brandeis. The Warren Court charged the NAACP Legal Defense Fund with answering original-intent questions about the framers of the Fourteenth Amendment: what evidence existed that Congress or the states "contemplated or did not contemplate, understood or did not understand, that it would abolish segregation in public schools"? And as a further charge the court asked whether, if Congress and the states didn't understand this at the time, the framers of the Fourteenth understood that a future Congress might have the power to abolish segregation. When Thurgood Marshall asked Franklin's help, he gave intensely of his time. As he wrote: "I wrote historical essays, coordinated the work of some of the researchers, and participated in the seminars that the lawyers held regularly."[12] He pored over the minutes of the 1865–1866 Joint Committee on Reconstruction, debates in Congress and in the state legislatures, private correspondence of key figures, and a survey of public reactions and response to events of the day in Washington.

The conclusions he reached were that the pre–Civil War views of the radical abolitionists dominated the thinking of the framers of the Fourteenth and, therefore, the original egalitarian intent of the framers had been frustrated and vitiated by the separate-but-equal doctrine erected in 1896. "*Original intent* of the Fourteenth Amendment had indeed been nullified," he reasoned, "by the actions of its enemies, who were racial segregationists"[13]—an interpretation subscribed to by the Constitutional historian Herman Belz but flatly rejected by legal historian Paul Finkelman. In the final analysis, the Supreme Court found the historical question "at best inconclusive" and based its decision in *Brown v. Board of Education* on contemporary cultural-psychological reasoning. But it may still be said that, in one sense, when the NAACP lawyers argued their *Brown v. Board* briefs before the Supreme Court, they had history on their side.

12. "A Life of Learning," in ibid., 287.
13. "The Historian and the Public Policy," in ibid., 313.

This story of historians and public policy has an interesting sequel. I have in mind Franklin's contribution to C. Vann Woodward's *The Strange Career of Jim Crow* (1955). For those who want the closest and most lucid reading of what Woodward says about the relatively late emergence of institutional segregation in the South and the furious debate the so-called Woodward thesis has sparked among historians, no better treatment exists than that found in John Cell's *The Highest Stage of White Supremacy* (1982). Woodward himself several times revisited and revised the argument in *Strange Career*. When it was first published, however, the book's considerable impact had clear public policy implications for American race relations, for if racial segregation was a recent juridical construct dating from the late 1890s, then it followed surely that stateways could indeed change folkways—that "all deliberate speed" should be both speedier and more deliberate. Such a conclusion, drawn from the careful scholarship of the dean of American historians, was of considerable value to the liberal forces of the 1960s. In his autobiographical memoir, *Thinking Back: The Perils of Writing History,* Woodward assigned much of the responsibility for the original argument in *Strange Career* to John Hope, his friend of many years. Alas, Professor Woodward later wondered about the wisdom of Franklin's counsel and his own insights and evinced a certain distaste for the presentism he permitted to color his interpretation. We who remain committed to those ends and their means that Lyndon Johnson would translate as affirmative action continue to note with appreciation Franklin's contribution to the strange career of C. Vann Woodward.

Historians, a German philosopher once sniffed, are prophets in reverse. Looking back over the career of John Hope Franklin, one can espy a trajectory arcing in the later years out of history into law and public policy and now, it appears, into the privilege of prophecy. His 1993 book, *The Color Line: Legacy for the Twenty-First Century,* might be said to be inspired by Santayana's well-worn premonition about the past and his student Du Bois's repeatedly invoked admonition about the future. Reviewing the national spoilage of the Teflon Presidency, Franklin took on the new conservatives with a vengeance and forecast many of the dire consequences of our continual evasion as a country of the costs of poverty and racism. Writing as a moralist who is a historian, he enjoins us at the end of this provocative little book: "Perhaps the very first thing we need to do as a nation and as individual members of society is to confront our past and see it for what it is. . . . Having done that, we should then make a good-faith effort to turn our history around so that we can see it in front of us, so that we can avoid doing what we have done for so long."[14]

John Hope Franklin is shining proof that history, as Henry Ford once said, is not bunk. We honor ourselves in praising him and we close with a paraphrase of a soldierly saying: Old historians never die, they just make history.

---

14. *The Color Line: Legacy for the Twenty-First Century* (Columbia: University of Missouri Press, 1993), 74.

The Scholarship of John Hope Franklin

GEORGE M. FREDRICKSON

$\mathcal{O}\!\!\!\int$ HAVE BEEN assigned an almost impossible task—to survey and evaluate John Hope Franklin's scholarship. Since he published his first article more than sixty-five years ago, he has produced at least thirteen original books, almost as many edited volumes, and dozens of essays, twenty-seven of which he considered worth collecting for the volume *Race and History,* published in 1989. Obviously I can do no more than scratch the surface of this monumental achievement. Franklin is probably best known for *From Slavery to Freedom: A History of Negro Americans,* first published in 1947 and now in its eighth addition. Translated into six foreign languages, it stands unchallenged as the standard history of the African American experience. He also authored a groundbreaking account of the Reconstruction era in American history. His *Reconstruction after the Civil War,* published in 1961, was the first book-length study by an academic historian to emphasize the positive aspects of the first national effort to establish equal rights for African Americans. Without being polemical or tendentious, it demolished the

19

stereotypes about the era that still prevailed at the beginning of the civil rights movement—the images of venal carpetbaggers, disreputable scalawags, hapless blacks, and oppressed southern whites that had been set forth by adherents of the Dunning school.

Among his other notable works are his biography of the pioneer African American historian George Washington Williams, published in 1985; *The Militant South,* a study of the mentality that led white southerners to secede from the Union and provoke a civil war, published in 1956; and *A Southern Odyssey: Travelers in the Antebellum North,* published in 1976. The last two books reveal something that Professor Franklin has often stressed about the subject matter of his work. He has refused to be ethnically pigeonholed as a black historian of black America. His real subject, he has insisted, is the history of the American South, white and black. An enemy of racial segregation in all its forms, he opposed the establishment of autonomous black studies programs and has consistently favored the integration of African American history into the historiographical mainstream rather than its isolation on the fringes of American history or, alternatively, its absorption into a transnational Afrocentric narrative. To his way of thinking, self-imposed scholarly separatism perpetuates Jim Crow rather than furthering the cause of black liberation.

What do I take to be the most important distinguishing features of Professor Franklin's scholarship? First and most conspicuous in this era of postmodernist relativism is his consistent and uncompromising commitment to factualism and the pursuit of scholarly objectivity. He believes that the primary obligation of the historian is to establish what actually happened in the past; in other words, that there is such a thing as historical truth and that we can find out what it is—not all of it perhaps but a significant portion. This factualist and objectivist commitment requires weighing all the evidence in a detached, dispassionate way and distinguishing between what is definitely true and what is only likely or possible. It also requires letting the chips fall without contaminating the process by wishful thinking, partisan didacticism, or tendentious theorizing.

To some younger historians such an orientation may seem epistemologically naive and hopelessly old-fashioned. But it is, I am convinced, the reason John Hope Franklin's scholarship has an enduring quality that is not likely to be attained by work that is more attuned to changing philosophical and historiographical fashions. His first book, *The Free Negro in North Carolina, 1790–1860,* published in 1943 and based on his Harvard doctoral dissertation, reads with as much authority today as when it was first published. It covers the subject so thoroughly and dispassionately that it remains, and will presumably remain for a long time to come, the definitive treatment of the subject. Only the discovery of a mass of new primary sources would be likely to reopen the topic. Would it have been better, do you think, if the book had preached or theorized in ways that might now seem dated, rather than letting the facts speak for themselves? Of course the facts can only speak for themselves after they have been selected, arranged, and imaginatively interpreted. But the creative historical imagination must be disciplined by proper historical method rather than allowed to range freely.

Professor Franklin's most recent book demonstrates his resistance to relying on highly subjective sources that can be readily employed to support a preconceived interpretation. *Runaway Slaves*—coauthored by Loren Schweninger—relies primarily on such contemporary documentary sources as newspaper accounts, advertisements, and court records in an effort to determine how often, under what circumstances, and with what consequences slaves absconded from the plantations of the Old South. Franklin and Schweninger make little use of two kinds of sources that have become very influential in slavery studies—the published narratives of those exceptional fugitives who made it to the North and the interviews with elderly ex-slaves recorded by the WPA writers' project in the 1930s. The former were likely to have been shaped by the polemical purposes of an abolitionist movement that relied heavily on the horrific testimony of escapees, and the latter relied on the uncertain childhood memories of people in their eighties or nineties, besides being conditioned by interview situations that may have discouraged candor. (The interviewers were often white southerners who were in effect asking during the height of the Jim Crow era about how their forebears might have treated the people they were interviewing.)

A good illustration of John Hope Franklin's willingness to confront historical facts that may be inconvenient for the purposes of inspiring our contemporaries to greater activism can be found in his 1961 book on Reconstruction. Although the main thrust of the book is to legitimize the civil rights movement by discrediting pro-segregationist myths about what occurred between 1865 and 1877 and why it was necessary to "redeem" the white south from "black domination," the picture that it presents of the black leadership of the period is less than exemplary by the standards of the 1960s. Based on his knowledge of what they actually said and did, Franklin concludes that, by and large, the politicians and community leaders who represented the African American community were surprisingly moderate and accommodationist in their attitude toward southern whites. While seeking the right to vote and hold office for themselves, they generally opposed the disfranchisement of ex-Confederates (a policy that was favored by southern white Republicans, whether carpetbaggers or scalawags). Furthermore, they did not strongly oppose segregation per se. Integration of schools and places of public accommodation was not high on their agendas, and relatively little was done during Reconstruction to go beyond legal and political rights in the narrow sense and toward social or economic equality. The black leadership of the Reconstruction era did not even oppose the laws on the books prohibiting interracial marriage. Sixties activists and others seeking a usable past in the form of historical models to follow were bound to be disappointed by the lack of black militancy that was revealed in *Reconstruction after the Civil War.* Some other histories written during the civil rights and black power eras professed to find a stronger anticipation of 1960s militancy in the 1860s, but they were unpersuasive and have largely been forgotten. Much of the scholarship of the late 1970s and beyond has tended to support the Franklin image of a cautious and moderate leadership, although this recognition has sometimes been accompanied by explicit disapproval of the elite as a self-serving middle class and an identification with the allegedly betrayed masses of black workers and sharecroppers. Professor Franklin might agree on some abstract level with such ideological judgments, but he would not regard it as within his mandate as a historian to render them.

John Hope Franklin's commitment to the more rigorous standards of historical accuracy and scrupulousness, the ethic of scholarly restraint that I have elsewhere described as an "austere professionalism," does not mean that he has been lacking in ideological passion and conviction. Far from it. The paradox that I would like to explore in the remainder of this essay is how he can be a fervent and effective proponent of racial equality and justice and at the same time a practitioner of detached, objective, and dispassionate historical scholarship.

One possible way to resolve the paradox might be to say that he writes or expresses himself in two genres—in professional historical writing and in other forms of expression in which he is fulfilling his role as a citizen or, as he himself put it somewhat facetiously I think, "blowing off steam in literary efforts." Although he has kept it out of his scholarship, the anger at how he and other African Americans have been treated has come to the surface from time to time when he has been able to put aside his professional historian's persona. One example is the set of lectures he gave in 1992 at the University of Missouri in a series on "the science of ethics" (published in 1993 as *The Color Line: Legacy for the Twenty-First Century*). Since ethics and not history was the subject, he seemingly found it easier than in most of his writings to address contemporary policy issues and render moral judgments. The main thrust of his argument is that the claim made by conservatives and others that racism is dead and that we have achieved a color-blind society is in fact the new face of American racism. "Unfortunately," he writes, "the litigation, the legislation, and executive implementation . . . did not wipe away three centuries of slavery, segregation, and discrimination. . . . Those who insist that we should conduct ourselves as if [a color-blind society] already existed have no interest in achieving it and would be horrified if we even approached it."

But I don't think we can bifurcate the passionate defender of racial equality and the careful, objective scholar quite so neatly as the "dual genre" or "multiple hats" thesis would tempt us to do. This is not the time or the place to confront epistemological questions concerning the nature of truth and knowledge, but it is possible in my opinion to accept the postmodernist notion that everyone is ideological, even the most objective and empirical historian, without drawing the extreme relativist conclusion that all ideologies are equal and that there is no certain way of distinguishing truth from falsehood. Whether it is self-evident truth instilled by our creator or a pragmatic belief system that can only be validated by what we can make happen in the future, the Enlightenment's ideal of human rationality and its conception of knowledge as the result of controlled, open-ended investigation (the scientific method or as close as we can come to it) would seem to lie at the root of both the historical practice and the egalitarian passion of our distinguished honoree. Slavery and segregation, he emphasizes in much of his historical work, were sustained by a set of demonstrable falsehoods about African Americans. The distorted and propagandistic picture of what happened during Reconstruction, which he has done so much to correct, served as a rationale for disfranchisement and Jim Crow in the late nineteenth and early twentieth centuries. Implicit in his conviction that truth—including historical truth—is naturally and inevitably the enemy of racism is a belief that honest, objective history contributes to the achievement of racial justice and equality simply by telling the truth and shining light into the dark corners of prejudice, greed, and hypocrisy. Partisan or polemical history, on the other hand, even if it seems to be enlisted in a good cause, will in the end impede it, because its factual distortions or omissions will inevitably be revealed.

Also implicit in this commitment to truthfulness and factuality is a belief in a human rationality and capacity to communicate that transcends and ultimately annihilates racial and ethnic divisions. John Hope Franklin's lifelong rejection of black separatism and race-based nationalism, his persistent affirmation of the *possibility* and *desirability* of the kind of color-blind society that it is so dangerous and misleading to believe already exists, is based on the assumption that a dedication to reasonableness and truth-seeking can break down barriers based on race or ethnicity. Even if you believe that such convictions are themselves a product of faith or ideology rather than being absolutely true for all time, we still might agree that they point to a possible future for humanity, a better world that our efforts as citizens and scholars might help to bring into existence.

The Scholar as Activist

ROBERT L. HARRIS, JR.

$\mathcal{QJ}$N MY REVIEW of "First Person Singular: John Hope Franklin," the Public Broadcasting System video that aired in 1997,
I wrote that John Hope Franklin "has been more than a public intellectual. He has been an activist scholar, with an abiding interest in
public policy and social change."[1] Dr. Franklin, in one of his early
essays, published in *Phylon,* posed the question:

> What is the field and function of history? Is it more than a
> bizarre account of the deeds of men? Is it the "shape of things
> that have been," with no particular meaning for those of us
> who live today and face the problems of a complicated world?
> Or could history itself be a manifestation of the inexorable
> march of man toward a better and finer civilization? As a mat-
> ter of fact, history has been all of these things and infinitely
> more. Its field and function have, unfortunately, been limited,
> expanded, and misdirected in the hands of so-called "Masters"
> of the trade who would define its status in terms of their own,
> sometimes evil, predilections.

1. *Journal of American History* 85:3 (December 1998).

He explained further that the historians who practiced their craft "with a view to exciting national, racial, or religious hatred have not only stamped indelible marks of shame upon their profession, but have also performed a revolting disservice to humanity."[2]

He published this essay, "History—Weapon of War and Peace," during World War II, a personal time of joy and sadness as he wrote in "Their War and Mine" in 1990. By 1940, he had married his college sweetheart, and he completed his Ph.D. degree in history the following year, at age twenty-six. It was a time of great joy. But experiencing the sting of American racism also made it a time of sadness. Given the outbreak of war in Europe and the reinstatement of the draft in the United States, Dr. Franklin answered an advertisement in his local newspaper that described a shortage of navy personnel with experience in typing, taking shorthand, operating simple business machines, and carrying out other office duties. Such qualified men, the advertisement promised, could look forward to early promotion. Dr. Franklin eagerly went to the recruiting office and proudly listed his qualifications, which included not only a Ph.D. from Harvard but also three gold medals in typing, six years of experience as a secretary in college and graduate school, an accounting course in high school, and proficiency in shorthand. Although he was highly qualified and the recruiter might have rejected him as overqualified, he was turned down and told flatly that the reason was due to his race. Because of this encounter and other indignities, he studiously avoided the military during World War II.

Dr. Franklin was pleased with the outcome of the war, especially the defeat of Nazism with its doctrine of Aryan supremacy, but he thought that the United States had been hypocritical in proclaiming its fight for democracy and egalitarianism abroad, while oppressing its own citizens at home. He supported the "Double V" campaign that the *Pittsburgh Courier* promoted for victory at home in dismantling segregation and abroad in defeating fascism. He regretted

2. "History—Weapon of War and Peace," *Phylon* 5:3 (1944): 249, 252–53.

the internment of Japanese Americans in concentration camps during the war and the use of the atomic bomb, which made the United States the first country in the world to use "weapons of mass destruction." His *Phylon* essay was an effort to influence the writing of history for the cause of peace rather than as an instrument of war. His observations some sixty years ago are especially timely as this nation experiences the aftermath of a war with Iraq, begun allegedly for the purpose of preventing the use of "weapons of mass destruction" that this country introduced to Iraq in the first place. In 1944, Dr. Franklin observed, "In the relations of mankind, the settlement of differences in a civilized and peaceful way is the only way that is in the direction of perfection. As a social discipline, the historical process should, it seems, be forged into a mighty weapon for the preservation of peace."[3]

He saw history not only as a weapon for peace but also as a means to forge a better society in the United States. He described the United States as a country that from its beginning displayed two contradictory ways of life. The country embraced a democratic and liberal tradition that emphasized human dignity, while it denied many of its inhabitants a place within that tradition. He challenged historians to use "their art as a weapon for the destruction of what obviously is one of our most besetting sins and which more than once has threatened our own civilization." Dr. Franklin was not asking for a usable past that distorted history for a cause. He held that the dispassionate, impartial, and judicious approach of the historian with a commitment to truth could influence America's march toward freedom and democracy for all her citizens. He maintained that the historian had a responsibility to preserve and to promote the best features of American society.[4]

In "First Person Singular," Dr. Franklin explained that he consciously decided to become a revisionist historian, to set the record

3. Ibid., 255.
4. Ibid., 256.

straight, especially about southern history. The prevailing interpretation of southern history cast the South as a region that had been prostrated by the Civil War, Emancipation, and allegedly corrupt black rule during Reconstruction. Dr. Franklin, as consummate scholar, challenged that interpretation. He has shed light on the past to improve race relations in this country. But he has not confined himself to only one side of the story. When writing African American history, he has written about whites as well as blacks. And when writing American history, he has infused it with the humanity of black people. History, like the orchids that he cultivates, helps us, he has commented, to understand variation and to provide new interpretations and different ways of viewing the past. Ultimately, the past should help us in the conduct of our lives in the present and in the future. For Dr. Franklin, the United States is an enterprise that has involved the contributions of many people, and it is the historian's job to reveal the rich tapestry of their lives.

He has observed, however, "The path of the scholar is at best a lonely one. In his search for truth, he must be the judge of his findings and he must live with his conclusions. The world of the Negro scholar is indescribably lonely; and he must, somehow, pursue truth down that lonely path while, at the same time, making certain that his conclusions are sanctioned by universal standards developed and maintained by those who frequently do not even recognize him."[5] Although these words were written many years ago, when black scholars had limited access to libraries, grants, and research universities, have things changed that much for the black scholar today? Is scholarship on African Americans accorded the same weight as work on other topics? Are historians of the African American past basically working on the margins of the discipline of history? Dr. Franklin was determined to become not just a black historian but a historian who happened to be black. In that determination, he has

---

5. "The Dilemma of the American Negro Scholar," in *Race and History: Selected Essays, 1938–1988* (Baton Rouge: Louisiana State University Press, 1989), 304.

been guided by the highest standards of scholarship, while also rendering great service to his race and to his country. He has not lived in an ivory tower, cloistered from the people and problems outside the academy.

Unfortunately, today, as William M. Banks has noted in *Black Intellectuals: Race and Responsibility in American Life*, "With the lowering of formal racial barriers, black intellectuals feel free to reject any identification with the black community at large, free to sidestep the troublesome questions posed by ongoing racial inequality. Under the elegant banner of individual freedom, the new individualists ask whether it is fair to expect black intellectuals to act differently from white intellectuals and to assume a larger burden than they."[6] I do not think that Dr. Franklin ever saw working actively to improve black America as a dilemma. From his participation in the American Council on Human Rights during the late 1940s and early 1950s, his preparation of documents on the meaning of the Fourteenth Amendment for the *Brown v. Board of Education* Supreme Court case, his chairmanship of the Joint Center for Political Studies' Committee on Policy for Racial Justice, to his chairmanship of President William J. Clinton's Initiative on Race, and much work in between in the struggle for human and civil rights, Dr. Franklin has been more than a public intellectual; he has been an activist scholar.

Identification and valorization of the black public intellectual is rather recent. Robert S. Boynton, in an *Atlantic Monthly* article, helped to popularize the rise of the "new" black public intellectual, with a nod to the contributions of earlier black public intellectuals such as Alain Locke, W. E. B. Du Bois, St. Clair Drake, E. Franklin Frazier, and, of course, John Hope Franklin.[7] The new black public intellectuals emerged with the growth of the media and a need to address the conundrum of race in America. The rise of an educated black public created a need for information and perspective on

6. *Black Intellectuals: Race and Responsibility in American Life* (New York: W. W. Norton & Co., 1996), 245.
7. "The New Intellectuals," *Atlantic Monthly* 275:3 (March 1995).

current events.[8] The new black public intellectuals were primarily literary critics, social scientists, humanists, and legal theorists. Their commentary addressed cultural expression and to some extent public affairs.[9] Few historians appear on lists of the new black public intellectuals because historians generally do not publish as much in the popular media. Moreover, Michael Berube has suggested that the new black public intellectuals' focus on culture and cultural criticism has not influenced the more practical areas of education, employment, and public welfare.[10]

Richard A. Posner, in a much debated new book, defines "public intellectuals as intellectuals who opine to an educated public on questions of or inflected by a political or ideological concern."[11] Posner has compiled perhaps the first comprehensive statistical survey of public intellectuals for the twentieth century, living and dead. He lists 546 public intellectuals who have a "presence" in current American social thought. His list is based on the number of times that web sites have been consulted for specific names; the frequency of media citations for individuals as determined by LexisNexis databases of major newspapers, magazines, and radio/television news programs; and scholarly citations from science, social science, and arts and humanities indexes from 1995 to 2000. There are twenty-six African Americans on the list, or about 4.8 percent of the total, and fifty-seven historians, or about 10.4 percent of the total. For the top one hundred public intellectuals by media mention, there are only seven African Americans (three of whom are deceased). John Hope Franklin is one of those seven. Only five historians made this list, and Dr. Franklin is one of them.

8. Gerald Early, "Race and the Public Intellectual," in Saleem H. Ali, ed., "Beyond the Ivory Tower: Public Intellectuals, Academia and the Media" (draft manuscript at www.mit.edu/~saleem/ivory).

9. Alford A. Young, Jr., "Political Engagement and African American Scholars in the Age of African American Intellectual Celebrity," in Rutledge M. Dennis, ed. *Research in Race and Ethnic Relations: The Black Intellectuals,* vol. 10 (Greenwich, Conn.: JAI Press, 1997).

10. "Public Academy," *New Yorker* 70:44 (January 9, 1995).

11. *Public Intellectuals: A Study in Decline* (Cambridge: Harvard University Press, 2001), 2.

Public intellectuals, according to Posner, however, are more pontificators than doers, more social critics than constructors of social change. And it is on these grounds that I suggest that Dr. Franklin is more than a public intellectual, that he is an activist scholar. He has been involved in movements for fundamental change in American society, whether they involved school desegregation, the human and civil rights struggle, or the pressing issues of our time, such as affirmative action, racial justice, the black family, educational opportunity, or the widening socioeconomic gap between the black middle class and those African Americans struggling for basic survival. In "The Nineteen Eighties: Prologue and Prospect," written with Kenneth Bancroft Clark, Dr. Franklin observed, "The growing gap between the black middle class and the black underclass is weakening the cohesion that once produced a civil rights movement in which blacks of all classes could work together. Upwardly mobile blacks ignore the real danger that their own progress could be threatened if the public mood becomes more reactionary."[12] That statement is as prescient today as it was when published in 1981. John Hope Franklin has not just written about public policy, he has influenced government action.

He has argued for the historian's role in the formulation of public policy not in justifying certain actions after the fact but in explaining how historical events provide background and insight for desirable change. In his own work with the NAACP Legal Defense Fund in challenging school segregation, he helped the Supreme Court to understand the meaning and intent of the Fourteenth Amendment to provide equal protection of the laws for all citizens, regardless of race. The historians who were called on for research provided the data needed by the lawyers to trace the evolution of the idea of equality as it was expressed in the Fourteenth Amendment. Dr. Franklin proposed that direct discussion of public policy issues among historians and the government officials responsible for the formulation

12. "The Nineteen Eighties: Prologue and Prospect" (Washington, D.C.: Joint Center for Political Studies, 1981), 19.

and implementation of public policy might keep decisions more in line with public interest than with bureaucratic tradition. The historian brings perspective and critical evaluation to the issues of the day. He has suggested that the historian as a servant of the past is the conscience of the nation. "It is the function of the historian," he explained, "to keep before the people, with as much clarity as possible, the different lines of action that have been taken, the several, often complicated reasons for such action, and to point to the conflicts and inconsistencies, the contradictions and illogicalities, and to the defects and deficiencies when they exist."[13]

As chairman of the President's Initiative on Race, Dr. Franklin wrote to President Clinton each month during hearings that were held around the country. He provided recommendations on actions that could be taken immediately rather than waiting for the final report. Inspired by the appeal of a Latino from New Jersey, who drove to Dr. Franklin's home in Durham and described his complaint that had been languishing for three years before the Equal Employment Opportunity Commission (EEOC), Dr. Franklin advised President Clinton to increase the EEOC budget, which he subsequently did by $80 million to help with the backlog of complaints.[14]

John Hope Franklin is no newcomer to issues of human equality. He has been in the vanguard of efforts for human betterment and has used his sterling academic reputation in service to his country, his race, and his profession. To give you a sense of his endurance, when *Ebony Magazine* first published its list of the one hundred most influential Negroes in 1963, Dr. Franklin was among those listed. Thirty-nine years later, when the magazine published its most recent annual list of the one hundred most influential black Americans, there were only two individuals who appeared on the original list, Dorothy Height and John Hope Franklin. That is staying power!

13. "The Historian and the Public Policy," in *Race and History,* 319–20.
14. Ana Radelat, "Building One America in the Twenty-First Century?" *Hispanic* 11:12 (December 1998).

American Scholar and
Public Intellectual

WALTER B. HILL, JR.

I N T H E F A L L of 2001, Alfred Moss and I met to plan a plenary session on John Hope Franklin at the 2002 annual meeting of the Association for the Study of African American Life and History. Our intent was not only to create an opportunity for celebration and recognition but also to critically examine the man and his work. We believed that although the scholarly community had an obligation and responsibility to honor Franklin's enormous accomplishments, as well as his human decency, humility, and respect for the historical profession, there also ought to be an examination of why he is an American icon and an unusual American scholar and public figure. In the annals of the historical profession, there are many outstanding scholars who have made enormous contributions to the research and writing of American history. With all due respect to those great scholars, few, if any, have risen to the plateau that John Hope Franklin has reached.

For those of us baby boomers who attended undergraduate and graduate school or who became avid readers on the subject of African

American history, life, and culture, there is a good chance that the works of John Hope Franklin became a part of our reading. In the fall of 1968, I enrolled in Louis Jones's Afro-American History Survey 1 course at the College of Wooster in Wooster, Ohio. Jones had been trained at North Carolina Central University under a contemporary of John Hope Franklin, and a fine scholar in his own right, Earl Thorpe. As a young sophomore student with no declared major, I looked forward to taking my first black history course. Jones assigned his mentor's work, *The Central Theme of Black History,* but he also assigned John Hope Franklin's *From Slavery to Freedom.* Excited and enthusiastic, I consumed Thorpe's tantalizing essays. When I came to Franklin's *From Slavery to Freedom,* I could not put the book down. I immersed myself in the history, having never read anything like it before. The book was so well constructed, covering so many themes in black life, I believed I had learned everything I needed to know about black people and history. Some years later when I entered the classroom as a young history instructor, *From Slavery to Freedom* became my bible. The book embodied black culture to the fullest, and I wanted my students to be well grounded in John Hope Franklin. Even with the specialization and compartmentalization of American history, the book remains a fountain of knowledge for all students to draw from.

Any critical examination and assessment of African American historical scholarship will reveal the indelible imprint of the work of John Hope Franklin on American history. His work never took a doctrinaire position. It rarely if ever created theoretical frameworks and sought evidence to prove a point. His work has been void of outlandish assessments and conclusions, and it stayed away from using ideological formulations to make a statement. His work neither transposes other scholarship nor seeks out scholarship to further his conclusions. As a trained historian and senior archivist with the National Archives and Records Administration, I view scholarship through the eyes of both professions, and when I examine John Hope Franklin's work, I see sound, original scholarship at its best. His *The*

Emancipation Proclamation, published in 1963, remains one the best histories of the famous document and Lincoln's thought process in formulating it. There are several reasons *From Slavery to Freedom* is in its eighth edition and has sold more than three million copies. Most impressive, though, is the documentation, the fine use of historical evidence, and the superb use of scholarly language and style. The work remains one of the best-constructed general histories of African Americans.

John Hope Franklin is an unusual scholar. Baby-boomer scholars researched and wrote history with passion and mission, broke new ground, and turned history on its head, viewing historical processes from the bottom up. The times were ripe for it. With the civil rights movement, the black power revolution, Watergate, academic battles over black studies, the women's liberation movement, and Vietnam, the United States was an exciting place to be if you were a student of American history. The new themes and methods of doing history energized everyone as extraordinary scholarship emerged.

As we reflect on those times, we should pause to consider the source of John Hope Franklin's originality and genius, because he evolved in a totally different historical era. Certainly the new methodologies influenced his thinking about history, as was evident in his observations and comments on and participation in the turbulent but productive times of the 1960s and 1970s. I believe John Hope Franklin is an unusual scholar because he learned his craft in an era of virulent institutional and demonstrative racism. He emerged with an enlightened sense of integrity and truthfulness to his profession when he could easily have become an angry and ideologically bent political scholar—a scholar with a skewed view of race and history obsessed with proving the righteousness of African American history. Instead, from the very beginning he understood African American history as American history.

His *Race and History: Selected Essays, 1938–1988* is a testament to how he treated the subject. This is critical because John Hope Franklin, while writing about Negro Americans, understood their history as a part of the social fabric of America, yet he failed to quite fit the convention of "Negro scholar." Undoubtedly, he is in the tradition of Carter G. Woodson, Charles H. Wesley, Rayford Logan, and Benjamin Quarles. But I am not sure if he strictly defined himself as a Negro or a black scholar as those scholars did. He certainly made the choice to become a part of that particular historical tradition, but he also spoke to the broader issues of American history and scholarship that influenced the shape and fabric of American society. He discussed this position in his 1963 essay, "The Dilemma of the American Negro Scholar" (included in *Race and History*), concluding, "On the one hand, [the black scholar] joins those of his own color who seek to make democracy work. On the other hand, he joins his intellectual kinsmen of whatever race in the worthy task of utilizing the intellectual resources of the country for its own improvement."[1]

Jonathan Scott Holloway, in his fine work, *Confronting the Veil: Abram Harris, Jr., E. Franklin Frazier, and Ralph Bunche, 1919–1941*, raises a provocative question when he asks, "What are we to make of those intellectuals who, instead of conforming to a model of strict objectivity and academic cloakness, fashion their careers by being critical and actively engaged in the social worlds of their time?" John Hope Franklin anticipated Holloway's questions some decades earlier when he wrote in "The Dilemma of the American Negro Scholar," "It is, of course, asking too much of the Negro scholar to demand that he remain impervious and insensitive to the forces that seek to destroy his dignity and self-respect. He must, therefore, be permitted to function as vigorously as his energies and resources allow, in order to elevate himself and those of his group to a position where they will be accepted and respected in the American social order."[2]

1. *Race and History: Selected Essays, 1938–1988* (Baton Rouge: Louisiana State University Press, 1989), 308.
2. *Confronting the Veil: Abram Harris, Jr., E. Franklin Frazier, and Ralph Bunche, 1919–1941* (Chapel Hill: University of North Carolina Press, 2002); *Race and History,* 305–6.

As a scholar, John Hope Franklin clearly reflected a balanced, well-conceived, and poignant approach to the study of African Americans, American society, and American history. As a public intellectual, he asserted, engaged in dialogue about, and responded to criticisms of, a position contrary to the beliefs of mainstream America regarding race, historical truth, and social justice.

Following in the Footsteps
of John Hope Franklin

DARYL MICHAEL SCOTT

$\mathcal{MY}$ APPRECIATION for John Hope Franklin's scholarship has been an intellectual and professional journey. It began in the late 1960s as blacks as a people struggled for
rights and power. I grew up on the Southside of Chicago, where
everyone, or so it seemed, subscribed to group self-assertion and
political awareness. Back then, history lived. Slavery seemed as alive
as Jim Crow, and you would hear people talking about both, moving
back and forth through time as if everything was part of their personal experience. My encounter with Franklin's work was not love at
first reading. In my home, we had two histories of black people. We
had Lerone Bennett's *Before the Mayflower* and Franklin's *From
Slavery to Freedom.*[1] I was ten when I wrote my first history paper. It
was entitled "Abraham Lincoln, White Supremacist." It was a gloss
on Lerone Bennett's exposure of Lincoln's view that blacks could

---

1. Bennett, *Before the Mayflower: A History of Black America* (Chicago:
Johnson Publishing Co., 1962); Franklin, *From Slavery to Freedom: A History of
Negro Americans,* 2d ed. (New York: Knopf, 1956).

39

not be citizens and his desire to colonize us abroad.[2] History began for me as an eye-opener. Bennett's treatment of Lincoln had no counterpart in the way the Great Emancipator was spoken about or written about elsewhere. Bennett's revelation let me know that nothing could be received as truth. He made me a revisionist. In contrast, Franklin was too understanding of white people, too enamored of the American promise of equality. To be sure, he pressed the case for black equality, but he did so by affirming a myth. I was interested in the truth, and only those truths that could be placed in an indictment. Black people, I believed, needed to know their history, so they could understand the righteousness of their cause. In this endeavor, Bennett was the man.

Many years later, when I decided to pursue a doctorate, I continued to believe that the role of the black intellectual was to justify social change. At the same time, however, I had come to understand that scholars should have an additional function—to provide the vital information needed to affect the course of radical social change, if not revolution! It was at this moment that I began to realize the importance of Franklin's careful scholarship and the breadth of his learning. By the early 1980s, I believed that too many black historians were writing therapeutic histories that would liberate no one. If Franklin's black people suffered with dignity, black power historians saw resistance and heroism at every turn. It seemed that they never viewed historical knowledge as part of an inquiry aimed at understanding institutions and processes on their own terms so that weaknesses could be exploited and change could be effected. For them, as it had been for Bennett, history seemed to be useful only as a motivational tool or as a means of counting grievances. His lyrical prose notwithstanding, Vincent Harding's *There Is a River* did not lead to freedom, at least not in this world. To be sure, Franklin's work did not provide such analysis, but I was certain that his careful

---

2. Bennett revisited this topic recently. See his *Forced into Glory: Abraham Lincoln's White Dream* (Chicago: Johnson Publishing Co., 2000).

scholarship provided a model for inquiry. One needed only to ask different questions.

The more I took scholarship seriously, the more I appreciated Professor Franklin's achievements. Everywhere I turned, there he was. When I decided to learn more about free blacks, I encountered him. When I looked for a manageable history of Reconstruction, there he was again.[3] Everything I wanted to know about seemed to belong to him. It soon dawned on me that his *From Slavery to Freedom* had been a Herculean effort, for it did not rest on an enormous body of secondary sources. He had to dig the earth and pour much of the foundation himself. Having read Carter G. Woodson's work and having gone through every volume of the *Journal of Negro History*, I realized that in the 1940s Franklin's general history came from out of nowhere. Ever generous, Franklin has paid homage to the earlier efforts of scholars such as George Washington Williams, but it took much work and great historical imagination to fill out the historical record. At the time I realized this, I had tried my hand at an original paper or two, so I could recognize that he was a dedicated master of his craft. For all my ideological differences, I realized that I would do well to carry his note cards.

In the last two years, I've had the opportunity to do research in some of Professor Franklin's old haunts, and on a number of occasions I have thought about him and how things must have been under Jim Crow. While I was at Stanford, he told a group of us graduate students stories about his archival experiences. He told us that he had been denied access to the main reading room at North Carolina's State Archive in Raleigh and relegated to a separate room, where the archivists brought him research materials. Last year, I visited the Alabama State Archive and, operating with a faulty memory, mistook it for the scene of Professor Franklin's forced segregation. That assumption colored everything I saw. I assumed that the building

---

3. Franklin, *Reconstruction after the Civil War* (Chicago: University of Chicago Press, 1961) and *The Free Negro in North Carolina, 1790–1860* (Chapel Hill: University of North Carolina Press, 1943).

looked much as it had decades before, but nearly everything else had changed. The staff was now integrated, and so was the gallery of the state's great fathers. Among the busts was the likeness of Booker T. Washington. Reinforcing my own faulty memory with her own, an elderly white woman told me a story of how Franklin had been segregated at the archive. Sharing our common error, we went about performing our tasks in the new racial order: I handed her my call slips, and she had my requests retrieved and sent to a table at which we both believed Professor Franklin had been forbidden to sit.[4]

The obstacles notwithstanding, Professor Franklin and his integrationist coconspirators amassed a body of work that was political in its intent. Carefully and diligently they put before the world all the evidence needed to show how America had thwarted black people's efforts to enjoy their hard-earned freedom. The integrationist scholars fought the good fight, and they achieved much of their objective. Today we hear talk of intellectual dream teams, but I am not certain what game they are playing, let alone what they've won for black people. In contrast, the dream team on which Franklin played defeated segregation and opened countless doors. So successful were they that the present generation can either choose not to remember the past or, like me, afford to remember the narratives all wrong!

My generation of scholars also owes its intellectual freedom to John Hope Franklin. His stubborn insistence that he was an American historian provided a model for those of us who desire to write general history. If he made the case that American history could not be understood without the history of black folks, he also chided black scholars to recognize that black history can not be understood in a vacuum. When he voiced these concerns about black history in the 1960s, they were not popular. And I must confess, I thought they

4. After I delivered these comments, Franklin corrected me, pointing out that it was in North Carolina, not Alabama, that he had been segregated in the state archive. Leslie Harris of Emory University, who was present at dinner with me and Franklin in Palo Alto, California, later confirmed his recollection.

smacked too much of excessive integrationism. From the perspective of the 1970s, the need to rediscover the black past seemed more pressing than the need to try to understand white Americans, especially ethnic southerners. I knew all I needed to know about them. After twenty years of reading history, I can no longer find meaning in thinking of whites as racists and of ethnic southerners as the most extreme cases. That truth leaves me with less than a full measure of those people and the world in which my ancestors lived. I confess to being a little slow in my development, but by and by I made my way to where Franklin has been all long.

If John Hope Franklin has made all of American history his province, I am most indebted to him for what he taught me about our people. Even as I disagreed with his abiding faith in the ultimate soundness of American institutions, I could not help but admire his grasp of our ancestors' struggles. To be sure he focused on leaders and wrote as if the first slaves at the market were modern integrationists, but he never failed to miss the broad forces shaping black life. In recent years, the historiography of the progressive era has moved beyond the Washington–Du Bois debate. Although Franklin focused on the male leadership class, he made clear that the age of Washington was also the age of philanthropy. Recent studies that have emphasized the class and gender tensions in black life during the period would do well to rediscover how the black leadership class, accommodationist or militant, male or female, found it necessary to scramble for the support of powerful and wealthy white men and their wives. Any trend in the literature that moves too far away from his treatment of the period is moving away from bedrock truth.

Like all great scholars, Franklin has influenced the scholarship of successive generations, of individuals not directly connected to him. Those of us who train students know that we do not have to assign his books for our students to get the benefit of his scholarship. To cite one example, his work on free blacks in North Carolina comes through in everything I write or say about free blacks and North

Carolina. Since reading his monograph, I have joined him in trying to understand the influence of liberalism in shaping black life in the state. While at Columbia, I asked a graduate student about the relationship between liberalism and black power in North Carolina. His response is now an outstanding dissertation. His answers are neither mine nor Franklin's, but the intellectual connection between his work and Franklin's is unmistakable.

For the better part of a century, African Americanists have stood on very broad shoulders. Few scholars have made major contributions to primary research over so many decades, and fewer still have been so generous and gracious. When President Clinton needed someone to lead a national discussion on race in America, he chose the best person. But in calling this stalwart from the first dream team back into service, I think he got more than he hoped for, and everything we could have wanted.

The Professor as Mentor

GENNA RAE MCNEIL

$\mathcal{I}$N *THE STATE OF Afro-American History: Past, Present, and Future,* a timely and important volume edited by Darlene Clark Hine and published in 1986, John Hope Franklin wrote these words:

> Every generation has the opportunity to write its own history, and indeed is obligated to do so. Only in that way can it provide its contemporaries with the materials vital to understanding the present and to planning strategies for coping with the future. Only in that way can it fulfill its obligation to pass on to posterity the accumulated knowledge and wisdom of the past, which, after all, give substance and direction for the continuity of civilization.
>
> [For finally,] . . . when one begins . . . a history, one must be optimistic about its completion and about what it seeks to teach. If one believes in the power of his [or her] own words and in the words of others, one must also hope and believe that the world will be a better place by our having spoken or written those words.[1]

---

1. Darlene Clark Hine, ed., *The State of Afro-American History: Past, Present, and Future* (Baton Rogue: Louisiana State University Press, 1986), 49, 58.

John Hope Franklin—the scholar, the teacher, the advocate—sat behind a large desk at the University of Chicago listening to a young woman with a sizable "Afro" hairdo, dressed entirely in black, down to her lace-up boots, proudly wearing a "Free Angela Davis" button. He heard about how graduate school could not supersede work in Chicago's black communities, where the student was volunteering as secretary to Chicago's "Coalition," a black liberation coalition headed by the civil rights activist Rev. C. T. Vivian, but including Fred Hampton with the Black Panthers, Chicago's "youth nations," and others committed to the struggle against racist oppression. Professor Franklin heard a passionate argument about the need for blacks to write and teach our own history. He heard, finally, the plea that he make an exception for this young black woman and rather than having her combine southern history with another United States subfield, agree to direct her in Afro-American history, a subsidiary field within United States history that was not yet listed in the University of Chicago's graduate catalog as an available concentration or minor for the Ph.D.

I—yes, I was the young woman—shudder to think now what Professor Franklin must have been thinking as he patiently awaited the conclusion of these remarks. Even to me, these remarks seemed to continue without the speaker taking a breath, let alone leaving a moment for Professor Franklin to get the proverbial "word in edgewise." When I did conclude, Professor Franklin paused to reflect before he spoke. Yes, he would direct me in my studies of African (then Afro-) American history, but it would require, he forewarned, many independent reading courses, additional readings in connection with other courses, and an unswerving commitment to making the sacrifice to study when being in the community might feel like a greater contribution. He concluded by saying, "I will teach you. I will give you the tools to do history. Your job is to get the tools. You may then use them to write whatever you wish."[2]

2. The meeting took place after September 1969 but before the assassination of Fred Hampton. No notes were taken; Professor Franklin's exact words may have been "write whatever you choose."

Little did I know that in 1963 John Hope Franklin had penned these words:

> It is, of course, asking too much of the Negro scholar to demand that he remain impervious and insensitive to the forces that seek to destroy his dignity and self-respect. He must . . . function as vigorously as his energies and resources allow, in order to elevate himself and those of his group to a position where they will be accepted and respected in the American social order.[3]

As a graduate professor and dissertation adviser, John Hope Franklin could be depended on to be there for his students as they navigated the obstacle course called graduate school. Generous with his time, his talent, his vast knowledge, and his sources, he communicated in no uncertain terms that to become a scholar of history required a commitment to training that was specific with respect to research, reading, writing, teaching, and the handling of evidence. He was an exacting taskmaster who demanded each student's best but never used harsh criticism, demeaning comments, or negative reinforcement. He did not speak of racism as an excuse for anything, but he seemed to acknowledge the context in which African American students struggled to achieve. He could honor our pain while demanding our perseverance and the achievement of our personal best.

One lesson I learned in graduate school that has stayed with me throughout my life is the importance of learning one's craft and honing one's skills. Professor Franklin, in essence, required that we internalize the meaning of doing our jobs as historians. As he challenged himself to painstaking research and precision in communication, so did he set such a standard for his students. He taught us to understand that the sheer complexity of human life and behavior—the raw material with which historians must work—presented sufficient

3. "The Dilemma of the American Negro Scholar," in *Race and History: Selected Essays, 1938–1988* (Baton Rogue: Louisiana State University Press, 1989), 305–6.

difficulty as we searched for truth, and such difficulty was not to be compounded with avoidable failures.

Over the years, John Hope Franklin taught us to survey the field of history and understand what earlier historians did within their periods, even when we disagreed entirely with their conclusions. Our best response to that which was false or wrong would always be better scholarship, more painstaking research, deeper probing, and more complex thinking about the multifaceted nature of human experiences in this land. As a consequence, the standards never dipped below excruciatingly high.

Yet I believe that part of what Professor Franklin was teaching us is what Howard Thurman explained in his essay "A Sense of History."

> The truth is that we are never able to get our hands on all the facts in a given situation; something that is important always escapes our consideration and may lead us to a false conclusion honestly arrived at. The fact that it is honestly arrived at may not alter the fact that the conclusion is false. We are all creatures of limitation. . . . This does not mean we are excused for our errors due to lack of knowledge, experience or patience. But it does mean that even when we have done our best thinking, our most honest probing of our motives, plumbed the depths of our innermost cumulative experience of living, we may arrive at a point less than right. If this is true, then carelessness in attitudes, slovenly thinking, half-hearted attempts at understanding, all these are simply without justification. *Each person is under an obligation to do, to the limits of his powers, the very best thinking of which he is capable, as he faces even the simplest alternatives of life.*[4]

All of this Professor Franklin taught and did as a professor of graduate students. Even afterward, however, once I had become an assistant and then an associate professor myself, I recall his effort to

4. Howard Thurman, *Deep Is the Hunger—Meditations for Apostles of Sensitiveness* (1951; reprint, Richmond, Ind.: Friends United Press, 1973), 21–22. (Emphasis mine.)

be a nurturing mentor and wise counselor who compassionately listened to my account of the experience of being the only black on the faculty. My mentor, my counselor, he refused to permit me to make unwise comparisons between others' accomplishments and my own work.

Racism and sexism render this world quite messy, oppressive, and often mean. On more than one occasion he reminded me that each scholar seeks to produce his or her scholarship in a very specific context. He sometimes related the challenges he had faced, which he would later describe in his volume *Race and History.* He emphasized as well, however, the blessings of his life, chief among which was a wife who made their home a space where whenever he needed he could focus without interruption on his scholarship. Wonderfully warm, considerate, loving, and very bright, Aurelia Whittington Franklin handled the quotidian—meals, bills, household matters—as well as reading, proofreading, offering constructive criticism every time he shared with her his work. Aurelia Franklin took care of the details related to hosting graduate students at the Franklin home, and she fed me even when she was not supposed to be hosting students in her home. This she did as she initially pursued her own career as a highly skilled librarian and, later, as she managed a demanding schedule of other activities in addition to motherhood. Few are blessed to have such a partner in life, and for those who did not, Professor Franklin sensitively reminded us that scholarship is but one of the demands in life and that, even in regard to it, the concern must always be integrity of character and the work ethic we show within our own context.

Professor Franklin trained and mentored students of various ethnicities, but I would be remiss if I did not acknowledge that I and other African American women who attended the University of Chicago—such as Juliet E. K. Walker, Barbara Flint, Ruth Mason, and Nancy Grant—could depend on Professor Franklin for constructive criticism, recommendations, networking, advice, and concern long after we earned the Ph.D. and held our first jobs. I know he has pride in others, too, among them Darlene Clark Hine and Mary Frances Berry, whose careers he has watched and been willing to direct others' attention to, whether by writing a foreword or through a dedication in a book.[5]

As a teacher-scholar, John Hope Franklin has a remarkable work ethic that is consistent with his principles. In 1947 while at North Carolina College for Negroes (now North Carolina Central University), he completed and then offered *From Slavery to Freedom*, an African American history text, to a nation with far too little historical information about the experiences of African American people. As a part of the third generation of Afro-American historical scholarship that ended with the close of the decade of the 1960s, John Hope Franklin—along with Benjamin Quarles, Rayford Logan, Charles Wesley, Carter G. Woodson, Elsie Lewis, and others—chronicled African American achievements and the interactions of African Americans with white Americans. In each subsequent edition, Professor Franklin worked to meet his obligation to revise and update this general textbook to incorporate not only the recent past but also new knowledge derived from new scholarship. He did not seek to be the voice of another generation, but rather to hear those voices and—with former student Alfred Moss—to respond with diligent attention to omissions, comments, and criticisms as well as new insights. One cannot help but note that the work ethic of Professor Franklin is such that the eighth edition of *From Slavery to Freedom* not only updates the text in relation to current scholarship in the field but also responds specifically to commentary and critiques provided at the celebration of the fiftieth anniversary of the text. In so doing, for example, it bids the reader pay closer attention to African American women, expressive art, and resistance.[6]

Professor Franklin has taught and lived his beliefs about the duty

5. He provided the foreword to Darlene Clark Hine, *Hine Sight* (Bloomington: Indiana University Press, 1997), and dedicated *The Color Line* (Columbia: University of Missouri Press, 1993) to Mary Frances Berry.

6. The conference held in Durham at North Carolina Central University and Duke University in 1997 to celebrate the fiftieth anniversary of the text was

of the scholar, particularly in regard to what he has called "the obligation to pass on to posterity the accumulated knowledge and wisdom of the past, which, after all, give substance and direction for the continuity of civilization." The role of the scholar can be one of advising for both advocacy and policy formation, as long as one is clear about the difference between advocacy and scholarship. His work— as that of other historians who have influenced or continue to influence policy, such as Mary Frances Berry—provides substantial evidence of past practices and policies, their good effects and sometimes their folly. John Hope Franklin has always believed and taught that "it is the function of the historian to keep before the people, with as much clarity as possible, the different lines of action that have been taken, the several, often complicated reasons for such action, and to point to the conflicts and inconsistencies, the contradictions and illogicalities, and to the defects and the deficiencies when they exist."[7]

By precept and example, John Hope Franklin is a scholar who empowers, encourages, and challenges any scholar, but especially those who come out of a community of oppressed people, to "pursue truth" in one's scholarship with "a dedication and a commitment," to "maintain . . . the highest standards of scholarship," and to "persevere."[8] In large measure, long before I was ever taught or mentored by a woman of color who had earned a Ph.D., John Hope Franklin stood with me so that I might now say with Audre Lorde: "I have come to believe . . . that what is most important to me must be made verbal and shared, even at the risk of having it bruised or misunderstood."

In the transformation of silence into language and action, it is vitally necessary for each one of us to establish or examine

---

sponsored by both institutions and coordinated by a joint committee of administrators and selected faculty from NCCU and Duke and selected history faculty from UNC–Chapel Hill.

7. "The Historian and the Public Policy," in *Race and History,* 319–20.

8. "Dilemma of the American Negro Scholar," in *Race and History,* 304, 305.

her function in that transformation, and to recognize her role as vital within that transformation.

For those of us who write, it is necessary to scrutinize not only the truth of what we speak, but the truth of that language by which we speak it. . . . But primarily for us all, it is necessary to teach by living and speaking those truths which we believe and know.[9]

---

9. Audre Lorde, "The Transformation of Silence into Language and Action," in *The Cancer Journals* (Argyle, N.Y.: Spinster, Ink, 1980), 19.

A Perspective
from within the Family

How My Father Created the Context for My
Understanding of the African Diaspora

JOHN W. FRANKLIN

*G*ROWING UP in the Franklin household was an enriching experience. Living with my mother the librarian and my father the historian gave me access to information and a home-based library from which I could learn about the United States, the African American experience, European and Asian art, and African history and culture. When my reading for high school was not particularly stimulating, I went into my parents' library and read Du Bois, Countee Cullen, Jean Toomer, James Baldwin, and the Negro Caravan. My father read my essays and reports for school with care and much editing with red pens, which I can now appreciate.

Visitors from across the country and around the world would come for dinner, and through the discussions I would learn about many subjects and places. We entertained as a team, planning dinners at breakfasts prepared by Dad. His breakfast repertoire during my childhood was vast: catfish and grits, steak and eggs, western omelettes, codfish or salmon cakes, fried apples and bacon, latkes, pancakes and waffles, brains and eggs, kippers, scrapple, country ham with redeye gravy, and his very own turkey hash and grits with biscuits. I learned to cook from both of my parents, everything from down-home southern foods to frog's legs, beef bourguignonne, curries, and dals, but they blamed their high blood pressure and cholesterol on my free use of eggs, butter, and cream!

My parents loved plants, and we went from windowsills full of plants, to our window greenhouse for the first few orchid plants, to the rooftop nine-by-twelve-foot greenhouse, to a wide-body seventeen-by-fourteen one with a pond and two aisles.

I saw my father work every day, always writing something. I saw both of my parents work with community organizations, boards, museums, symphonies, and hospitals, and from them I learned how to give public service. I often went with my father when he was invited to speak about black history at churches of all denominations.

My wife, Karen, and I both grew up with the benefits of having older parents who were established in their careers and who broadened our horizons as theirs were broadened. With my parents I traveled to visit family and friends as well as for Dad to serve as a visiting professor at Cornell, Wisconsin, Berkeley, Hawaii, and Maryland. After several trips to Europe, some with my mother, he went to Nigeria, Zanzibar, and Kenya for their independence celebrations and brought us back real images and art from Africa. We lived in Cambridge, England, and visited Morocco, France, and Italy. I had the opportunity to see how people lived in different places, how prejudice of some form could be found everywhere, and how people fought injustice. I was exposed to Judaism and to Islam. My parents encouraged my interests and explorations. I then traveled on my own, to France, where I lived with a French family and attained early fluency. As a family we went to Trinidad as the guests of the prime minister, a former colleague of my father's from Howard University. In Trinidad, Dad lectured and collected orchids, and then we went on to Jamaica and Barbados. I went to Yugoslavia and Germany and back to England. I met people of African descent in Europe and then studied where they came from. At the suggestion of my professor St. Clair Drake, I studied with Aimé Cesairé in Martinique and made my first sub-Saharan swing through Ghana, Côte d'Ivoire, Liberia, and Senegal. I moved to Senegal for eight years, and my parents came to visit and took me with them to east, southern, and central Africa.

I moved back to Washington in the early 1980s for graduate school and have been working at the Smithsonian Institution in a number of capacities. By then my parents had left Chicago and moved back to Durham, North Carolina. My father was a dedicated husband and took care of my mother until her passing in 1999. In recent years, I have had the pleasure of working with my father on two projects. We edited *My Life and an Era: The Autobiography of Buck Colbert Franklin,* the autobiography of my grandfather, who was an attorney and writer in Oklahoma. We read from it at the National Book Festival, during the last peaceful weekend in September 2001. We worked with Renee Poussaint and Archbishop Desmond Tutu and twenty-one young people plus chaperons and a crew to film a documentary, "Tutu and Franklin: A Journey Towards Peace," in Senegal. With my wife, Karen, we now constitute a new traveling team. Following the filming in Senegal, we went to Brazil together in 2000 to celebrate the translation of *Race and History* into Portuguese. In 2001 we went to South Africa for the premiere there of "Tutu and Franklin."

Dad began working on his autobiography in 2000. It has been fascinating to learn in detail about his life before I came on the scene. Now that he is writing about the period when he is at Brooklyn College, I am learning what he and my mother experienced while I was growing up. We have spent much time together both in Washington and in Durham. He has agreed to advise me as I chair the Maryland Commission on African American History and Culture in Baltimore's Inner Harbor. We discuss the evolving discussion about the National African American Museum and whether it will or will not be part of the Smithsonian. My work takes me back and forth to Mali, where my office is working with the government of Mali and Malian scholars and culture bearers to plan the 2003 Smithsonian Folklife Festival. Dad told me that he has heard about Timbouctou since he was five years old and announced that he wants to visit there with me. So we are planning a trip in the not too distant future to go to one of the few places he has wanted to visit and has not seen, embarking on another journey of discovery, encountering people we have known elsewhere and meeting new people together.

The Black Collectivity and the Culture of Struggle

DARLENE CLARK HINE

ISTORIANS ARE guardians and purveyors of our nation's past (the past of both nations: that of the larger American society and that of the black collectivity).[1] We who are engaged in this work traffic in the commodity of Truth(s). No courier has been more significant in this trade than John Hope Franklin. I write this brief essay in part to express love and admiration for John Hope Franklin, but also to thank him for a body of impeccable scholarship that forced America to confront its racial past.

It is easy to savor and applaud the ingenuity, fresh and thoughtful insights, and depth of research that characterize each of John Hope Franklin's books. Here I am thinking in particular of *The Militant South, 1800–1861* (1956), *Runaway Slaves: Rebels on the Plantation*

---

1. By *black collectivity* I am referring to people of African descent who because of their historical experiences with global dispersal, slavery, segregation, discrimination, and disfranchisement forged a sociopolitical culture that encouraged and applauded struggle, resistance, and individual achievement to meet the needs of the people burdened by American racism.

(1999, coauthored with Loren Schweninger), and his award-winning *George Washington Williams: A Biography* (1985). While we appreciate the clarity of exposition and the superb craftsmanship undergirding the monumental bounty of his scholarship, it is equally imperative that we discern and acknowledge the determined and very human spirit behind them.

During the past one and a half centuries, black Americans have developed a complex, sophisticated, and, in many ways, extraordinarily effective culture of struggle. The writing and teaching of a black history that challenged and corrected prevalent stereotypes and distortions was central to the decades-long struggle for first-class citizenship and equality of opportunity. Joining John Hope Franklin in the early stages of the intellectual opposition to racism were historians Carter G. Woodson, Lorenzo Greene, Helen Edmonds, and Benjamin Quarles, to name but a few. The black collectivity was forged by a history of slavery, racism, and sexism; by terrorism and violence; and by relentless economic exploitation. As important as were the external forces that generated the collectivity, so too were the internal dynamics that gave it definition, coherence, and a semblance of real and imagined power.

As individuals and in groups, the black collectivity founded social and political organizations, as well as educational and professional institutions; engaged in migrations; underwent proletarianization and urbanization; and created artistic bulwarks (visual, written, oral, and performance). Some of its members wrote books and founded religious and cultural establishments that enriched our arsenal of survival strategies. Each individual member of the collectivity had the obligation to enter into, and the choice (made consciously or through serendipity) of how to shape and transform, the culture of struggle. Many in the black collectivity chose political activism; others collaborated and accommodated, or turned inward to operate within religious realms. Most black men and women resolved simply to persevere, to establish and nurture families while eking out a living within the constricted areas of the capitalist economy reserved for black people. A few pursued the artistic route and created a profoundly rich heritage of music, art, literature, and films that articulated and celebrated the souls and strivings of the black collectivity. Men and women in every station of life raised the status and ensured the survival of the black community as they met everyday needs. The members and leaders of the black professional and business entrepreneurial class advanced the ongoing liberation agenda by developing their unique talents.

All participated in and contributed to the culture of struggle in myriad ways. The farmers, washerwomen, and Pullman car porters were just as important as the lawyers, physicians, and professors. They were all part and parcel of the complex whole. To be sure, not all black Americans relished being members of this black collectivity. Some sought escape from the burden of race through passing, cynicism, alienation, and self-destruction.

My goal as a historian is to understand and illuminate the lives, work, and consciousness of a particularly small strata of African Americans. I investigate the experiences and contributions of those who became learned professionals: lawyers, physicians, nurses, and scholars. It is with this objective in mind that I pay tribute to the prolific and path-breaking historian John Hope Franklin. One strategy for coming to grips with the life and work of a scholar and activist whose career spans six decades is to situate him at the forefront of the culture of struggle of the black collectivity.

We study and revere John Hope Franklin because he has received a degree of prominence, recognition, and universal acclaim accorded to no other black historian in our lifetimes. Others have been celebrated in death. We are blessed to have the opportunity to pay homage to him in life. Our gratitude and accolades must in no way signal an absence of critical scrutiny, even though the more we know the more we discover how much there is to cherish in the life and work of this exemplary historian and gentleman who is John Hope Franklin.

John Hope Franklin is clearly one of the nation's most significant

American, southern, and black historians. In 1947 he authored the seminal text in the field of African American history. More than fifty years later, through eight editions with sales exceeding three million copies, *From Slavery to Freedom* represents the extent to which a book may become an institution in its own right. *From Slavery to Freedom* is one of the three pillars upon which rests the culture of black history. Another pillar is composed of academic and professional associations, such as the Association for the Study of African American Life and History; black studies departments and graduate history programs; the *Journal of Negro History* (now the *Journal of African American History*); and the annual Black History Month celebration. Actually, Black History Month is the bridge that connects the academic and professional to the third pillar. This is the public domain, a sphere that includes various museums, libraries, films, magazines, arts, and exhibitions.

Coursing through the culture of black history is a quite specific black history ideology that posits that knowledge of the past is an important source of empowerment that fuels resistance, encourages reform, and serves as the foundation of revolutionary transformation. In other words, contemporary social injustice and economic exploitation have deep roots in the American racial regime: slavery, Jim Crow/institutional racism, segregation, disfranchisement, and violence—physical, psychological, economic. Before it could be dismantled and ultimately destroyed, America's racial regime had to be destabilized and deconstructed. Black culture and history and the larger ongoing freedom movement challenge unspoken assumptions and repudiate allegations of black people's inferiority and limited intellectual capacity that are used to justify or rationalize racial exclusion and subordination in American society from slavery and in freedom.

Although there have been white scholars who made major contributions to the black history movement, clearly the chief architects were/are members of the black collectivity. John Hope Franklin's work spans four generations of black historians, none of whom stood more firmly than he did against the racial regime.

For more than six decades, Franklin's historical monographs, synthetic works, and biographical studies received critical acclaim from African American and white historians who heralded the interpretative challenges he launched against accepted negative analyses of black capacity. Let me review the evaluations of a few of his many books in order to underscore how generations of historians have benefited from his magnificent contributions to American historical scholarship.

Two of his most significant synthetic books were *Reconstruction after the Civil War* and *The Emancipation Proclamation.* Edgar Allan Toppin in a review of *Reconstruction* exclaimed, "Here at last is a judicious assessment of the controversial Reconstruction era. It is the best summary available, especially in fitting Southern developments into proper perspective with national issues." In this well-documented work, a model of remarkable constraint, Franklin demolished William A. Dunning's exaggeration of alleged "black rule" and the suffering of former white Confederates during the turbulent era. Historian Hans L. Trefousse declared *Reconstruction* "a most significant work which no one interested in the field will be able to overlook." Benjamin Quarles applauded Franklin's "many fresh slants" on the Reconstruction story. "For example, the typical Southern Negro that emerges from his pages is not the corrupt politician or the swaggering militia man, but an unheralded responsible head of a family, carrying himself with a new self-respect, as befitting one no longer a slave."[2]

Franklin followed the publication of *Reconstruction* with an equally provocative study of the Emancipation Proclamation. His boldly revisionist interpretation that Abraham Lincoln's concern about losing the war and not the destruction of slavery moved him to issue one of the most significant documents in world history is now conventional wisdom. He earned ardent praise from black historians who heralded him for introducing "new information" and "new

2. Toppin, *Journal of Negro History* 47. no. 1 (January 1962): 57–59; Trefousse, *American Historical Review* 67, no. 5 (April 1962): 745–46; Quarles, *Journal of Negro Education* 31, no. 1 (Winter 1962): 38–39.

interpretations" that blazed "new paths" and introduced "new personalities." Roland C. McConnell embraced Franklin's argument. He put it succinctly, "The Negro soon came to regard the Emancipation Proclamation as a symbol of complete freedom, begun now and to be completed in the future."[3]

While four generations of American historians took cues from Franklin's insightful, meticulously researched, and gracefully written scholarship, the black studies generation became more aware of him in the 1980s with the publication of his *George Washington Williams: A Biography*. In a review, C. Tsehloane Keto thought it "fitting and timely" that Franklin had written the first book-length study of the "flawed but brilliant" pioneer historian, George Washington Williams (1849–1891), the author of *A History of the Negro Race in America* (1882) and *History of Negro Troops in the War of the Rebellion* (1887). Keto marveled at the four decades of research in the United States, Zaire, and the Belgian Congo that went into the book's preparation, concluding, "Running down all the pieces of information on George Washington Williams alone would have been sufficient to make this biography a notable one." A particularly important contribution of the biography was Franklin's discussion of Williams's 1890 journey to the Congo and the inclusion (as appendixes) of three letters and reports that William wrote criticizing the "cruel and oppressive" treatment of the Congolese by the Belgian government. Deborah Gray White in a lengthy and thoughtful review of the biography declared, "Thanks to John Hope Franklin, Williams will not be as easily ignored in the future as he was in the past." Waldo F. Martin Jr. similarly intoned, "By powerfully illuminating the intricate contours of that commitment [to "the dignity as well as the rights of darker peoples everywhere"] and legacy, Franklin's superb biography dramatically recaptures the man, his times, and his significance."[4]

3. *Journal of Negro History* 48, no. 4 (October 1963): 298–300.
4. Keto, *Journal of Black Studies* 17, no. 4 (June 1987): 513–15; White, "Resurrecting a Historian," *Reviews in American History* 15, no. 1 (March 1987): 78–83; Martin, *Journal of American History* 73, no. 2 (September 1986): 483–84.

In addition to his remarkable body of scholarship, Franklin has consistently raised his voice against discrimination and segregation. He assisted Thurgood Marshall's team of lawyers, social scientists, and historians in gathering evidence that informed the historic U.S. Supreme Court *Brown v. Board of Education* (1954) decision. He embodies the scholar as social activist and inspired generations of us to never accept less than the full human dignity guaranteed by the U.S. Constitution and captured so well in the Declaration of independence. His scholarship and his life reveal as much about the past as they teach us about living responsibly in the present. I always believed there was something special about the fact that his middle name is Hope. Thanks to John Hope Franklin, we of the black collectivity who internalize the meanings of his life, and strive to continue on the course toward truth and justice that he blazed, anticipate an even brighter future for all human beings.

Continuing Mentor

LOREN SCHWENINGER

IT IS A PLEASURE and an honor to comment on John Hope Franklin's influence and impact on American history. Many are aware of his numerous honors and awards, his long stream of articles and books, his involvement in the judicial and political reforms of the twentieth century, and his remarkable professional attainments, including the presidency of the Organization of American Historians. Many are also aware of his many contributions as a scholar, writer, critic, and observer of the human condition. Some are, perhaps, acquainted with his personal qualities. He is a man of warmth, compassion, humor, understanding, humanity, intellectual rigor, intense personal loyalty, grace, equanimity, and elegance.

I would like to offer, with your indulgence, three personal anecdotes that illustrate some of these qualities.

In October 1996, I was invited to introduce John Hope at an awards ceremony at Saint Augustine's College, in Raleigh, North Carolina, where he had taught many years before. After discussing his years at Fisk and Harvard, his early publications, including his 1938 article in the *New England Quarterly* entitled "Edward Bellamy and the Nationalist Movement," I talked about his influence on his students at the University of Chicago. "Having arrived at the University of Chicago and enrolled in his History of the South course *thirty years ago almost today,*" I began, knowing that the audience would be impressed by how long our student-teacher relationship went back, "I found his class electrifying." As I took his other classes over the years, and served as his research assistant, it became clear how fortunate I was to have such a mentor. As a teacher, he was generous with his time, positive, encouraging, demanding, and inspiring. Concluding, I again emphasized how long ago this had been—*thirty years*—and how his lessons still remained vivid in my memory. When I sat down and as Professor Franklin walked across the stage to begin his remarks, a gentleman in the audience stood up and in a strong voice said: "John Hope Franklin was my teacher too. I wish to thank him for all he did for me. I was a student in his class here at St. Augustine's in 1941!"

A second incident occurred the following year, in 1997, in Durham, North Carolina, at a party hosted by Myrna Adams, an administrator at Duke University who was laying the groundwork for the creation of the John Hope Franklin Center for Interdisciplinary and International Studies. During 1997 and early 1998, I journeyed from Greensboro to Durham about every other week to spend three or four days working with John Hope revising the manuscript for our forthcoming book, *Runaway Slaves: Rebels on the Plantation.* This party occurred during one of those visits. (I should mention parenthetically that this was an extremely enjoyable time and, despite Professor Franklin's extensive travels as chair of the advisory board to One America, the President's Initiative on Race, we missed only one scheduled writing session.) Back to the party. As it ended, a group of about twenty-five people sat in a circle around a large table. At one point in the conversation, the hostess asked John Hope if he had, on any earlier occasion, cowritten anything with me. With a twinkle in his eye John Hope said: "Only his dissertation."

Third, many years earlier, in the spring of 1969, as a graduate student I was given the great honor of taking care of John Hope's orchids for five days while he and Aurelia were out of town. The instructions were clear: water certain plants on certain days; keep the humidity at 50 percent; keep the temperature at 72+ degrees; make sure the heater and fan are functioning; and sprinkle the plank floor with water daily. Then, as we were about to step out of the greenhouse (located off the third floor of his townhouse on Blackstone Avenue in Hyde Park), he pointed to a beautiful blooming pale red and pale pink orchid, with its tiny-petaled flowers not a half-inch across. Holding it delicately in his hand, he marveled at its beauty and told me it was one of his newest acquisitions, shipped to him following a recent trip abroad. Three days later, as I was attending to my duties, I accidentally knocked the pot with the tiny orchid onto the plank floor, breaking it into many pieces. The peat moss and bark dropped irretrievably between the planks. The delicate bare roots of the orchid stared up at me. My heart dropped to my stomach. Would I be able to continue in graduate school? What should I do? Should I put the plant in another pot and not say anything about it? What if it died? In the end, I tried to replant it the best I could and awaited the Franklins' return. Even as they came through the door I thought, "I won't tell him." Finally, I mustered up the courage and explained what had happened. He neither winced nor frowned but merely said, "Oh, don't worry. Orchids are hardy plants. I'll repot it in the morning."

These three episodes suggest, at least in a small measure, the remarkable spectrum of students over six decades who claim Dr. Franklin as their teacher, the many additional books and articles he could have written had he not been so determined that his thirty-four doctoral students would produce clearly written, solidly researched dissertations, and that despite his incredible productivity over so many years, people have always been more important to him than things, even a beautiful orchid.

From Slavery to Freedom

A Work Always in Progress

ALFRED A. MOSS, JR.

I N 1947, when I was four years old, the first edition of *From Slavery to Freedom* was published by Alfred A. Knopf. The author, of course, was John Hope Franklin, then professor of history at North Carolina College for Negroes, now North Carolina Central University. The year that first edition appeared, reviewers and commentators almost invariably characterized Professor Franklin as "a Negro historian." Today, there is a broad consensus among historians that this label, along with kindred terms such as *black historian,* or *African American historian,* is too parochial to describe the work of this great scholar.

For Professor Franklin used *From Slavery to Freedom,* and his many other writings, to redefine our understanding of American history and give shape and focus to an emergent special field of American history, which we describe today as African American history and African American studies. On the fiftieth anniversary of the publication of *From Slavery to Freedom* in 1997, historian David Brion Davis described it as a work that "helped to evaporate racial segregation and oppression" by giving rise "to a reexamination of American history and how it was recorded." And, as historian Leon Litwack declared in an article published in 2002, Franklin "is an African-American historian, a Southern historian, an American historian. Just as he broke the color line in Southern archives as a graduate student, so he broke that same color line in Southern studies as a writer and teacher, moving from the largely segregated field of Negro history (as it was then called) to Southern history, an exclusively white domain."[1]

There are many ways to trace the evolution of Professor Franklin's seminal work, *From Slavery to Freedom*. One is through examination of the prefaces to the first five editions. As he was for the first edition, Professor Franklin was the sole author of the second through the fifth editions, which were published in 1956, 1966, 1973, and 1979, respectively. Each contained new information, as well as revised interpretation, flowing from his and others' research.

In the preface to the first edition, dated April 4, 1947, Professor Franklin told his readers that "in the present work I have undertaken to bring together the essential facts in the history of the American Negro from . . . [the] ancient African beginnings . . . to the present time." The author had, in his words, "made a conscious effort" to write the history of people of African descent in North America and the United States, "with a continuous recognition of the mainstream of American history and the relationship" of African Americans to it. Professor Franklin's approach was based, he wrote, on the assumption "that historical forces are all-pervasive and cut through the most rigid barriers of race and caste." It is, he reminded his readers, "impossible to trace the history of the Negro in

1. Davis, in [Durham] *Carolina Times*, August 23, 1997, p. 5; Litwack, "The Road from Rentiesville: The Greatest Historian of the Black Experience in America Speaks of What Has Changed during His Long Life, and What Has Not. An Interview with John Hope Franklin," *American Heritage* 53 (February–March 2002), p. 1 on Internet reprint.

America without remaining sensitive to the main currents of American civilization," or to the "interaction" between African Americans and the "American environment."[2]

Professor Franklin described the narrative of the book as a "balance between recognizing the deeds of outstanding persons and depicting the fortunes of the great mass" of African Americans, for, as he observed, "the history of the Negro in America is essentially the . . . [history] of the strivings of the nameless millions who have sought adjustment in a new and sometimes hostile world. This work is, therefore, a history of the Negro people, with a proper consideration for anonymous as well as outstanding people." The first preface to *From Slavery to Freedom* also expressed gratitude, in the words of its writer, to the "scholars who have contributed significant writings to this field." With particular thanks, he mentioned by name four great scholars who had been pioneers in the field of African American history: Carter G. Woodson, Charles H. Wesley, W. E. B. Du Bois, and Luther P. Jackson.[3]

In the preface to the second edition, Professor Franklin wrote briefly about the ways in which he drew upon his various ongoing research and writing projects, as well as the flood of new scholarship, to expand, refine, and improve this edition of the book. He also expressed gratitude to the book's many "careful readers" for their help in pointing out "errors and oversights."[4] Similar statements would appear in the prefaces to the third, fourth, and fifth editions. Continuous research, careful attention to the emerging relevant scholarship, and a responsive ear to readers, who constantly brought new information to his attention, became fixed patterns that informed the subsequent revisions and expansion of *From Slavery to Freedom*. These procedures contributed to the power and

---

2. "Preface to the First Edition," in John Hope Franklin and Alfred A. Moss, Jr., *From Slavery to Freedom: A History of African Americans,* 7th ed. (New York: Alfred A. Knopf, 1994), xxi–xxii.

3. Ibid., xxii.

4. "Preface to the Second Edition," in ibid., xxix–xxx

authority of the work and, with each new edition, renewed its appeal and expanded its readership.

What was less visible was the enormous amount of time, energy, and creativity required to draw upon these myriad sources, something I could not appreciate fully until I joined Professor Franklin as his coauthor on the sixth edition. One of my first tasks as we began to work together was to help with reading the seemingly endless river of correspondence that flowed steadily into his office from scholars sharing articles, books, newly unearthed documents, and unpublished papers. Along with these letters came ones from individuals in the United States and abroad sharing information that often added significant content to some aspect of African American history. But to talk about being Professor Franklin's coauthor at this point is to get ahead of myself.

The prefaces to the first five editions of *From Slavery to Freedom*, as well as the content of those volumes, make it clear that this was a work in progress. From edition to edition it evolved, informed by Professor Franklin's prodigious research, which drew on the ever-expanding body of documents, articles, and books addressing the history of blacks in North America and the United States and, equally significant, his convincing interpretation of the meaning and importance of these sources.

The period from 1947 to 1979, the years during which the first five editions appeared, was one in which, both inside and outside academic institutions, the discussion of African American history was closely related to some of the fiercest political debates in the United States. Professor Franklin's commitment to balanced scholarship and carefully reasoned judgment insured that *From Slavery to Freedom* did not became a pawn of those acrimonious debates. This must have disappointed some, possibly many, of his readers, perhaps prompting his statement in the preface to the third edition, dated July 4, 1966, that *From Slavery to Freedom* "is a history and not a contemporary tract."[5]

5. "Preface to the Third Edition," in ibid., xxvii.

In the preface to the fifth edition, dated May 30, 1979, Professor Franklin commented on the momentousness of the thirty-two years since the appearance of the first edition. He pointed to the mid-twentieth-century black civil rights movement as an event "with far-reaching impact on virtually every aspect of life" among African Americans, "one that has affected their position in American society as well as the manner in which other Americans view them." Drawing the attention of his readers to the challenge he had faced in attempting to evaluate so recent and so controversial a series of events, he described his efforts to guard against "distortion and exaggeration." As readers of the fifth edition of *From Slavery to Freedom* know, he met the challenge splendidly, presenting a brilliant discussion of what he described as "The Black Revolution."[6] Resting on comprehensive research, his treatment was balanced and carefully reasoned, while at the same time provocative and challenging.

With the publication of the sixth edition of *From Slavery to Freedom* in 1987, forty years after the first edition was issued in 1947, my name appeared for the first time as coauthor. Although both authors shared in the drafting of the preface to this edition, as they would in the writing of everything that appeared in this and subsequent editions, Professor Franklin provided the five sentences that explained why he had invited me to join him as coauthor:

> Two considerations have led to some major changes in the preparation of the Sixth Edition. . . . One has been the growing diversity of interests as well as the increasing complexity of the problems facing [African Americans]. This has required the constant monitoring and evaluation of virtually everything that occurs. The very magnitude of the task beckons more than one mind and one set of hands. The other is that with the passage of time, the original author has recognized the need for the collaboration of a younger person

6. "Preface to the Fifth Edition," in ibid., xxiii–xxiv. The term *Black Revolution* was first used in the fourth edition. In the third, *Negro Revolution* was used.

whose different perspectives and ample energies would assist
in giving the edition the freshness that it requires and de-
serves.[7]

These gracious and generous words obscure the intense intellectual energy, creativity, and personal drive that Professor Franklin
brought to the tasks of revising and expanding not only the sixth
edition, but also the seventh and eighth that followed in 1994 and
2000, respectively. So inexhaustible did Professor Franklin's "younger"
coauthor find him, that I was forced to ask, repeatedly, when were
we going to break for a rest, a walk, or, dare I even say it, a nap. After
all, as I quickly learned working alongside him in the two studies
and library of his home in Durham, North Carolina, my coauthor
was a person who rose regularly at 6:00 A.M. and, after a quick breakfast, followed by his brief spiritual commune with the orchids in his
greenhouse, was ready and eager to begin the day's work by 7:00 A.M.,
Saturdays and Sundays included. I should add that these workdays
frequently ended at midnight or thereafter. Indeed, there were a
number of occasions when I was forced to ask—with a completely
straight face—"Do you believe in lunch?" And I threw every bit of
my identity as an Anglican priest into the question. As I think back,
it's clear to me that this was a prayer as much as a request for information.

Permit me to step back in time now and write about the development of my relationship with John Hope Franklin. I first became
aware of Professor Franklin while still a boy, initially through comments made by my parents in praise of his writings. Both my father
and my mother were serious students of African American history.
As an undergraduate during the early 1960s, and while a student in
divinity school in the mid-1960s, I read Professor Franklin's books
and articles, becoming ever more appreciative of the great work he
was doing, both as a scholar and as a public intellectual.

7. "Preface to the Sixth Edition," in ibid., xxi.

Shortly after I arrived at the University of Chicago in 1968 to take up my duties as an Episcopal chaplain, I met John Hope Franklin for the first time and, with fascination, began to watch him from afar. Even though we had been introduced and were sometimes present at the same meetings or gatherings, he did not know me. Attending his public lectures and occasionally sitting in on classes he taught, I quickly became aware that he was as brilliant a teacher as he was a scholar. What also impressed me was his greatness as a human being—his personal and financial generosity toward worthy causes and his deep, genuine, caring interest in the welfare of others, regardless of a person's race, gender, importance, wealth, or education. To me, in a setting like the University of Chicago, where distinguished scholars were not always persons of morality, dignity, or humanity, Professor Franklin stood out as a true and shining star.

In 1970, I decided to begin work on a doctoral degree in history. The history graduate program at the University of Chicago was one of three at outstanding universities to which I applied, and I was fortunate enough to be accepted into all three. As part of a process for deciding which program and setting would be best for me, I visited all three (leaving Chicago for the last) and, at each, met the distinguished scholar who would be my adviser if I decided to study there. During my visit to Chicago's department of history, where Professor Franklin was then chairperson, I met with him and found him both gracious and welcoming. Nevertheless, for reasons I didn't fully understand at the time, I left still undecided.

Then, one evening, a few days before the date I had set for myself to say yes to one school and no to the others, I went, as part of my work as one of the University of Chicago chaplains, to an emergency meeting. The persons responding to the special call for this meeting came together to discuss ways in which we, as individuals and as a group, could work to stem a dramatic rise in crime, violence, and racial tension in Chicago. One of the people at that meeting was Professor Franklin. As the group of disparate individuals deliberated on a complex series of problems that seemed almost insoluble,

Professor Franklin played a major role in helping them develop a sense of common purpose and shared goals. When that meeting was over, I knew that I would be going to the University of Chicago to study history and, more important, to be a student of Professor Franklin's.

In 1985, ten years after I completed my doctoral work, to my surprise Professor Franklin invited me to join him as coauthor in researching and writing the sixth edition of *From Slavery to Freedom*. It was a signal honor and one that, initially, I found as intimidating as it was exciting. As I told a newspaper reporter in 1997: "I was overwhelmed when he asked me to work with him."[8] My first response was to tell him that I didn't know if I would be comfortable differing with him on issues related to research and interpretation because of my great respect for him. I suppose I was asking, indirectly, if our relationship could survive serious disagreements about significant matters. In response, he told me that my intellectual independence was one of the chief reasons he was extending the invitation to me. He wanted a coauthor who, in addition to being a serious researcher, with a genuine interest in ideas, would be honest and forthright in stating his agreements and disagreements. The only answer I could give to that response was: "Yes. Thank you."

Coauthoring the sixth, seventh, and eighth editions of *From Slavery to Freedom* has been a wonderful experience. I thank the author of the first five editions for the solid foundation he laid for our joint work together. Since the 1947 appearance of the first edition, the book has sold more than three million copies and been translated into Chinese, French, German, Japanese, and Portuguese.[9]

As Professor Franklin and I labored together to produce three editions of *From Slavery to Freedom*, I was humbled and inspired repeatedly by the fact that my coauthor is a person who, at the height of his success, is still seeking to learn, self-critical, tireless, and a

8. [Durham] *Carolina Times,* August 23, 1997, p. 5.
9. Kristen Mellitt (editor, McGraw-Hill Higher Education Division) to Alfred Moss, March 27, 2002.

fearless truth-teller. As Leon Litwack has so well stated, Professor Franklin

> is too good a historian to romanticize the [past]; he is too good a historian to replace old lies with new myths or with eulogistic sketches of heroes and heroines. He is too good a historian to subordinate history to ideology, to the polemical need of the present. He fully appreciates the ways in which race hustlers and ethnocentrists, white and black, have sought to use the past and how for more than a century the abuse of the past by historians and others helped to legitimize a complex of racial laws, practices, and beliefs.[10]

It is a rare privilege and a great gift to have been the student and to be the coauthor of one of the twentieth century's greatest scholars, intellectuals, and moral figures.

10. Litwack, "The Road from Rentiesville," 2.

A Collage of Tributes

JOURNAL OF BLACKS IN HIGHER EDUCATION

E DITOR'S NOTE: In 1997, to mark the fiftieth anniversary of the publication of *From Slavery to Freedom,* the *Journal of Blacks in Higher Education* asked leading historians of the Civil War and the American South to comment on the importance of the book and on the career of John Hope Franklin.

JOHN HENRIK CLARKE

I have been acquainted with Dr. John Hope Franklin for more than fifty years. I have been able to use his book *From Slavery to Freedom* in all the courses I have taught in African American history. This has led me to a consideration of his other books. In this field, he is considered to be black America's senior scholar.

CATHERINE CLINTON

From Slavery to Freedom was a landmark book that reflected the great promise and now symbolizes the powerful delivery of John

Hope Franklin: that he remains a scholar of immense insight and erudition, that he continues a researcher of indefatigable talent, that not only has he been a teacher who left his mark on his own generation but several future generations of American historians have profited by his example as well. Franklin has been a vital, dynamic voice for incorporation of the black experience into the great pageantry of the American past.

All of these stand as a remarkable testimony to Franklin's abilities, but many of us value his example as a colleague whose qualities recommend him as "a gentleman and a scholar," with no apologies to the fashions of the times which may scorn such appellation. He represents a standard to which younger talents aspire, exhibits an intense fascination with life—from the grit and grime of the academy to the hothouses where his beloved orchids thrive—and because of his spirit he has let a hundred ideas bloom in his wake, as his cultivation and creativity provide us with ongoing inspiration. We salute him as we remain in his debt.

DAVID BRION DAVIS

After many decades when American slavery was marginalized in most textbooks and other works on American history, John Hope Franklin's *From Slavery to Freedom* helped to restore the subject to its absolutely central place in the history of our nation. Like C. Vann Woodward's *The Strange Career of Jim Crow,* it coincided with the civil rights movement and helped to evaporate the racist myths that had upheld racial segregation and oppression.

STANLEY L. ENGERMAN

John Hope Franklin's outstanding contributions to American history have included such detailed monographs as *The Free Negro in North Carolina, 1790–1860; The Militant South, 1800–1861; Reconstruction after the Civil War; A Southern Odyssey: Travelers in the Antebellum North;* and *George Washington Williams: A Biography;* numerous essays and edited works; and that excellent and long-lasting textbook *From Slavery to Freedom: A History of Negro Americans.* After five editions, he joined with Alfred A. Moss Jr. for, to date, two editions. This book has undergone some revisions with the great expansion in the study of black history, and also considerable additions as important events developed in the post-1947 world, and the general historical approach and interpretations have maintained the highest standards of coverage and relevance. In addition to the lessons to be learned from the text and the great usefulness of the detailed bibliography, the brief prefaces, particularly that to the first edition which has been reprinted in succeeding editions, provide an excellent statement of how historians should undertake historical writing. This text has left its mark on historical studies, and its influence will no doubt continue.

ERIC FONER

In the fifty years since its publication, *From Slavery to Freedom* has introduced generations of students, as well as readers outside the academy, to the richness and drama of the African American experience, as well as making plain why no account of American history can be complete that does not accord African Americans a central role. Although not the first survey of black history (one thinks of the prior work of Carter G. Woodson, for example), *From Slavery to Freedom* has been by far the most influential, not least in forcing "establishment" colleges and universities to take African American history seriously as an intellectual endeavor.

The successive revisions, meanwhile, mirror both the expansion of scholarship on the black past and the changing currents of social and political thought within the black community. Overall, it is difficult to think of a "textbook" in any field of American history that has enjoyed so pervasive an influence as this.

GARY W. GALLAGHER

John Hope Franklin has been a leading figure in the field of American history for more than half a century. Few scholars can match his splendid contributions to the literature on southern, African American, and Reconstruction history, and fewer still can boast of a book that has reached a large audience over as many decades as has *From Slavery to Freedom*. The successive editions of this book alone would have guaranteed Professor Franklin's reputation; together with his vast body of other work, *From Slavery to Freedom* leaves untold scholars and students deeply in his debt.

HENRY LOUIS GATES, JR.

I first read *From Slavery to Freedom*—the black, thick, paperback edition—in February 1991, on a great riverboat sailing down the Congo River from Kisingani to Kinshasha in what was then called the Congo. I read it like a novel, straight through, cover to cover. As a pioneering feat of scholarship in African American studies, it has no precedent—none. My fondest dream would be to create a work of scholarship in the field of African American literature as germinal, as salient, as compelling, and as timeless as *From Slavery to Freedom*.

EUGENE D. GENOVESE

John Hope Franklin came upon the scene at a moment when the study of African American history cried out for synthesis and new directions. With *From Slavery to Freedom* and other works, Dr. Franklin provided the decisive guidance we needed. Simultaneously, he has emerged as a leading historian of American history in general, whose works are likely to remain required reading for generations to come.

WINTHROP D. JORDON

Fifty years!!! When I first read *From Slavery to Freedom* the book was only ten years old, but even by then it was a clear beacon built on solid rock. At the time, its field of inquiry was still marginalized by most members of the historical profession. But it continued to buttress the later historiographical explosion. That eruption has included shards of name changes—from Negro history, to black, to Afro-American, to African American—but these changes have done nothing to alter the fundamentally solid nature of the book as it too has changed along with major shifts in scholarly interests and discoveries.

Very few such books maintain their preeminence for such a long time. This persistence of high quality is, in my opinion, a direct reflection of John Hope's own personal qualities. If one set out to find a combination of courage in the face of terrible harassment, persistence in the cause of creative scholarship, grace in the face of high accomplishment, and generosity to others (especially younger scholars), one would find first a person whose name is John Hope Franklin.

PETER KOLCHIN

The life of this book corresponds to the life of African American history as an academic discipline. When *From Slavery to Freedom* first appeared, few took the study of black history seriously. Colleges and universities rarely employed specialists in the subject, and even more rarely employed African American scholars; except at historically black institutions, courses on black history were virtually nonexistent. Now that era seems remote: Even the smallest colleges offer such courses, major universities provide distinguished programs in African American studies, and so many books and articles appear on black history that it is impossible to keep up with them.

Although the growth of African American history as a discipline is not the product of one person's labors, John Hope Franklin has done more than any other living individual to make the field what it is today. As a pioneering scholar, as mentor to dozens of graduate students who went on to become professional historians themselves, as author of the textbook that remains, after fifty years, the standard in the field, he is rightly regarded as a Founding Father of African American history.

ROBERT K. KRICK

John Hope Franklin's classic is one of those books that inaugurated a new era of scholarship. After a half-century, it remains a standard, the direct lineal ancestor of the best that has followed.

JAMES M. MCPHERSON

For half a century, *From Slavery to Freedom* has been the best and most comprehensive single-volume history of African Americans. It is a valuable reference work; it is indispensable to teachers of black history; and it is a good read. May it stay in print for another half-century.

EDMUND S. MORGAN

John Hope Franklin was there before the rest of us and showed us the way. He is one of the few who have changed the contours of American history as we know it.

JAMES I. ROBERTSON, JR.

John Hope Franklin was the dean of Afro-American historians in 1947 when he published *From Slavery to Freedom.* The book won instant acclaim as the best general history of blacks in America. The passage of a half-century has only enhanced both reputations. More than that, to know Dr. Franklin is to have a genuine friend. He epitomizes everything that is good in the historical profession.

EMORY M. THOMAS

John Hope Franklin is one of the very few genuinely great people I have been fortunate enough to know. He sets my standard for qualities such as grace, integrity, dignity, generosity, class, charm, and, oh yes, brilliance. John Hope is my model of what a great intellectual should do and be.

C. VANN WOODWARD

During the fifty years I have known and read John Hope Franklin, I have expected the best from an American historian I admired, and I have never been disappointed.

Bibliography of the Published Works of John Hope Franklin

SUSAN KING

I. BOOKS

The Free Negro in North Carolina, 1790–1860. Chapel Hill: University of North Carolina Press, 1943. Reprint, Chapel Hill: University of North Carolina Press, 1995.

From Slavery to Freedom: A History of Negro Americans. New York: Alfred A. Knopf, 1947; 8th ed., 2000. Indian translation, 1973; Japanese translation, 1974; German translation, 1978; French translation, 1984; Portuguese translation, 1989; Chinese translation, 1990.

The Militant South, 1800–1861. Cambridge: Belknap Press of Harvard University Press, 1956. Reprint, Urbana: University of Illinois Press, 2002.

Reconstruction after the Civil War. Chicago: University of Chicago Press, 1961. Reprint, Chicago: University of Chicago Press, 1994.

The Emancipation Proclamation. Garden City, N.Y.: Doubleday, 1963. Reprint, Wheeling, Ill.: Harlan Davidson, 1995.

Land of the Free: A History of the United States, with John W. Caughey and Ernest R. May. New York: Franklin Publications, 1965. Rev. ed., New York: Benziger Bros., 1966.

Illustrated History of Black Americans, with the editors of Time-Life Books. New York: Time-Life, 1970, 1973.

A Southern Odyssey: Travelers in the Antebellum North. Baton Rouge: Louisiana State University Press, 1976.

Racial Equality in America. Chicago: University of Chicago Press, 1976. Reprint, Columbia: University of Missouri Press, 1993.

George Washington Williams: A Biography. Chicago: University of Chicago Press, 1985. Reprint, Durham, N.C.: Duke University Press, 1998.

Race and History: Selected Essays, 1938–1988. Baton Rouge: Louisiana State University Press, 1989. Portuguese translation, 1999.

The Color Line: Legacy for the Twenty-First Century. Columbia: University of Missouri Press, 1993.

Racial Equality in America & The Color Line: Legacy for the Twenty-First Century. Columbia: University of Missouri Press, 1994.

Runaway Slaves: Rebels on the Plantation, with Loren Schweninger. New York: Oxford University Press, 1999.

II. EDITED WORKS

The Diary of James T. Ayers: Civil War Recruiter. Springfield: Illinois State Historical Society, 1947. Reprint, Baton Rouge: Louisiana State University Press, 1999.

A Fool's Errand, by Albion W. Tourgee. Cambridge: Belknap Press of Harvard University Press, 1961.

Army Life in a Black Regiment, by T. W. Higginson. Boston: Beacon Press, 1962.

The Negro in Twentieth Century America: A Reader on the Struggle for Civil Rights, with Isidore Starr. New York: Random House, 1967.

Color and Race. Boston: Houghton Mifflin, 1968.

The Suppression of the African Slave Trade, 1638–1870, by W. E. B. Du Bois. Baton Rouge: Louisiana State University Press, 1969.

Reminiscences of an Active Life: The Autobiography of John Roy Lynch. Chicago: University of Chicago Press, 1970.

Black Leaders of the Twentieth Century, with August Meier. Urbana: University of Illinois Press, 1982.

African Americans and the Living Constitution, with Genna Rae McNeil. Washington, D.C.: Smithsonian Institution Press, 1995.

My Life and an Era: The Autobiography of Buck Colbert Franklin, with John Whittington Franklin. Baton Rouge: Louisiana State University Press, 1997.

III. CHAPTERS/CONTRIBUTIONS TO EDITED COLLECTIONS

"Reconstruction." In *Problems in American History,* edited by Arthur S. Link and Richard Leopold. Englewood Cliffs, N.J.: Prentice-Hall, 1952; rev. eds., 1957 and 1966.

"The Negro and the New Deal." In *The New Negro Thirty Years Afterward,* edited by Rayford W. Logan. Washington, D.C.: Howard University Press, 1955.

"The Democratization of Educational Opportunity." In *Issues in University Education: Essays by Ten American Scholars,* edited by Charles Frankel. New York: Harper and Brothers, 1959.

"Lincoln and the Politics of War." In *Lincoln for the Ages,* edited by Ralph Newman. Garden City, N.Y.: Doubleday, 1960.

"'As for Our History. . . .'" In *The Southerner as American,* edited by Charles Grier Sellers, Jr. Chapel Hill: University of North Carolina Press, 1960.

"Slavery and the Martial South." In *American History: Recent Interpretations,* edited by Abraham S. Eisenstadt. New York: Thomas Y. Crowell, Co., 1962.

"The Dilemma of the American Negro Scholar." In *Soon, One*

Morning: New Writing by American Negroes, 1940–1962, edited by Herbert Hill. New York: Alfred A. Knopf, 1963.

"The Integration of the Atlantic Community." In *The Atlantic Future,* edited by Henry V. Hodson. London: Longmans, 1964.

"The Past in the Future of the South." In *The South in Continuity and Change,* edited by John C. McKinney and Edgar T. Thompson. Durham, N.C.: Duke University Press, 1965.

"A Brief History of the Negro in the United States." In *The American Negro Reference Book,* edited by John P. Davis. Englewood Cliffs, N.J.: Prentice-Hall, 1966.

"The Emancipation Proclamation." In *An American Primer,* edited by Daniel J. Boorstin. Chicago: University of Chicago Press, 1966.

"Reconstruction and the Negro." In *New Frontiers of the American Reconstruction,* edited by Harold M. Hyman. Urbana: University of Illinois Press, 1966.

"The Two Worlds of Race: A Historical View." In *The Negro American,* edited by Talcott Parsons and Kenneth B. Clark. Boston: Houghton Mifflin, 1966.

"The Negro since Freedom." In *The Comparative Approach to American History,* edited by C. Vann Woodward. New York: Basic Books, 1968.

"Discovering Black American History." In *The Negro Impact on Western Civilization,* by Joseph S. Roucek and Thomas Kiernan. New York: Philosophical Library, [1970].

"Election of 1868." In *History of American Presidential Elections, 1789–1968,* vol. 2, edited by Arthur M. Schlesinger and Fred L. Israel. New York: Chelsea House, 1971.

"Ethnicity in American Life: The Historical Perspective." In *Ethnicity in American Life,* by the Anti-Defamation League of B'nai B'rith. New York: Anti-Defamation League, 1971.

"John R. Lynch: Republican Stalwart from Mississippi." In *Southern Black Leaders of the Reconstruction Era,* edited by Howard N. Rabinowitz. Urbana: University of Illinois Press, 1982.

"A Modest Imperialism: United States History Abroad." In *Guide to the Study of United States History outside the U.S., 1945–1980*, vol. 1, edited by Lewis Hanke. White Plains, N.Y.: Kraus International Publications, 1985.

"Effetti Sociali Delle Difference Regionali Negli Stati Uniti." In *Regionalismo e Centralizzazione Nella Storia Di Italia e Stati Uniti*, by Luigi De Rose and Ennio Di Nolfo. Florence: L. S. Olschki, 1986.

"Equality in America: Democracy's Challenge." In *A Melting Pot or a Nation of Minorities*, The Andrew R. Cecil Lectures on Moral Values in a Free Society, vol. 7, edited by W. Lawson Taitte. Austin: University of Texas Press, 1986.

"On the Evolution of Scholarship in Afro-American History." In *The State of Afro-American History: Past, Present, and Future*, edited by Darlene Clark Hine. Baton Rouge: Louisiana State University Press, 1986.

"Slavery and the Constitution." In *The Encyclopedia of the American Constitution*, edited by Leonard W. Levy. New York: Macmillan Publishing Co., 1986.

"The Desperate Need for Black Teachers: A Special Appeal from John Hope Franklin." In *Voices of Social Education, 1937–1978*, edited by Daniel Roselle for the National Council for the Social Studies, Washington, D.C. New York: Macmillan Publishing Co., 1987.

"Pursuing Southern History: A Strange Career." In *Developing Dixie: Modernization in a Traditional Society*, edited by Winfred B. Moore, Jr., et al. New York: Greenwood Press, 1988.

"The Moral Legacy of the Founding Fathers." In *Slavery, Revolutionary America, and the New Nation*, edited by Paul Finkleman. New York: Garland Publishing, 1989.

"The North, the South, and the American Revolution." In *Slavery, Revolutionary America, and the New Nation*, edited by Paul Finkleman. New York: Garland Publishing, 1989.

"Martin Luther King, Jr., and the Afro-American Protest Tradition."

In *We Shall Overcome: Martin Luther King, Jr., and the Black Freedom Struggle,* edited by Peter J. Albert and Ronald Hoffman. New York: Pantheon Books, 1990.

"African-Americans and the Bill of Rights in the Slave Era." In *Crucible of Liberty: 200 Years of the Bill of Rights,* edited by Raymond Arsenault. New York: Free Press, 1991.

IV. PUBLISHED ARTICLES AND ADDRESSES

"Edward Bellamy and the Nationalist Movement." *New England Quarterly* 11 (December 1938).

"The Free Negro in the Economic Life of Ante-Bellum North Carolina." Parts 1, 2. *North Carolina Historical Review* 19 (July/October 1942).

"Slaves Virtually Free in Ante-Bellum North Carolina." *Journal of Negro History* 28 (July 1943).

"History—Weapon of War and Peace." *Phylon* 5:3 (1944).

"Negro Episcopalians in Ante-Bellum North Carolina." *Historical Magazine of the Protestant Episcopal Church* 13 (September 1944).

"The Enslavement of Free Negroes in North Carolina." *Journal of Negro History* 29 (October 1944).

"James Boon, Free Negro Artisan." *Journal of Negro History* 30 (April 1945).

"George Washington Williams, Historian." *Journal of Negro History* 31 (January 1946).

"UN's Host." *Free World* (June 1946).

"James T. Ayers, Civil War Recruiter." *Journal of the Illinois State Historical Society* 40 (September 1947).

"Whither Reconstruction Historiography?" *Journal of Negro Education* 17 (fall 1948).

"New Perspectives in American Negro History." *Social Education* 14 (May 1950).

"Slavery and the Martial South." *Journal of Negro History* 37 (January 1952).

"Geschichte der Vereinigten Staaten in Andern Landern." *Aufklarung* (May 1952).

"From Slavery to Freedom." *United Asia* 5 (June 1953).

"Desegregation—The South's Newest Dilemma." *Listener* 54 (September 1955). Reprinted in *Journal of Negro Education* 25 (spring 1956).

"Sectionalism and the American Historian." *Atti Del X Congresso Internazionale Di Scienza Storiche* (September 1955).

"History of Racial Segregation in the United States." *Annals of the American Academy of Political and Social Science* 304 (March 1956).

"The New Negro History." *Crisis* 64 (February 1957). Reprinted in *Journal of Negro History* 42 (April 1957).

"Jim Crow Goes to School: The Genesis of Legal Segregation in Southern Schools." *South Atlantic Quarterly* 58 (spring 1959).

"The Southern Expansionists of 1846." *Journal of Southern History* 25 (August 1959).

"Lincoln and Public Morality." *Chicago History* (October 1959).

"The Negro's Dilemma." *New York Times,* January 17, 1960.

"To Educate All the Jeffersonians." *Superior Student* (April 1960).

"Freedom and Equality in a Pluralistic Society." *University of Melbourne Gazette* 26 (August 1960).

"A Century of Civil War Observance." *Journal of Negro History* 47 (April 1962).

"Civil Rights in American History." *Progressive* 26 (December 1962).

"First Century of Freedom." London, 1963.

"The Emancipation Proclamation, 1863–1963." *Crisis* 70 (March 1963).

"An Der Schwelle Zur Gleichberechtigung." Bad Godesburg, 1964.

"Before Ten Years Ago." *NAACP Freedom Journal,* New York, 1964.

"Indo-American Cultural and Educational Exchange, Some New Perspectives." *American Studies in India,* New Delhi, 1964.

"The Dignity of Man: Perspectives for Tomorrow." *Social Education* 28 (May 1964).

"Civil Rights and the Negro Poll." *Western Mail,* Cardiff, Wales, October 27, 1964.

"The Two Worlds of Race: A Historical View." *Daedalus: Journal of the American Academy of Arts and Sciences* 94 (fall 1965). Reprinted in *University of Chicago Magazine* (December 1965, January 1966).

"Freedom's New Frontiers." *Negro Digest* (September 1965).

"Pioneer Negro Historians." *Negro Digest* (February 1966).

"Freedom From Despair." *Chicago Today* 4 (winter 1967).

"The American Scholar and American Foreign Policy." *American Scholar* 37 (autumn 1968).

"The Bitter Years of Slavery." *Life* 65 (November 22, 1968).

"The Future of Negro American History." *New School for Social Research* (1969). Reprinted in *University of Chicago Magazine* (February/March 1970).

"John R. Lynch, Congressman from Mississippi." *Midway* 10 (autumn 1969).

"Archival Odyssey: Taking Students to the Sources." *American Archivist* 32 (October 1969).

"George Washington Williams and Africa." Inaugural lecture in honor of Rayford W. Logan, Howard University Press, 1970.

"Pubic Welfare in the South during the Reconstruction Era, 1865–1880." *Social Service Review* (December 1970).

"Perspective on the Holidays." *Tuesday at Home* (December 26, 1971).

"The Great Confrontation: The South and the Problem of Change." Presidential address delivered at the annual meeting of the Southern Historical Association, Houston, Texas, November 18, 1971. *Journal of Southern History* 38 (February 1972).

"Negroes and LBJ's Great Society." *Focus* (February 1973).

"The Next Hundred Years." *Detroit News,* October 7, 1973.

"The Historian and Public Policy." Address delivered as the Nora and Edward Ryerson Lecture. Center for Policy Study of the University of Chicago, 1974.

"The Enforcement of the Civil Rights Act of 1875." *Prologue: Quarterly of the National Archives and Records Administration* 6 (fall 1974).

"On the Oversupply of Graduate Students." *Daedalus: Journal of the American Academy of Arts and Sciences* (fall 1974).

"The Moral Legacy of the Founding Fathers." *University of Chicago Magazine* (summer 1975). Reprinted in *Current* (July/August 1975); *Tuesday Magazine* (September 14, 1975).

"The North, the South, and the American Revolution." Presidential address delivered before the Organization of American Historians, Boston, Massachusetts, April 1, 1975. *Journal of American History* 62 (June 1975).

"The Complete Historian." *Great Lakes Journal* 1 (1976).

"Libraries in a Pluralistic Society." American Library Association, 1977.

"The Historian and Public Policy." *History Teacher* 11 (May 1978).

"George Washington Williams and the Beginnings of Afro-American Historiography." *Critical Inquiry* 4 (summer 1978).

"Afro-American Biography: The Case of George Washington Williams." *Proceedings of the American Philosophical Society* 123 (June 1979).

"'The Birth of a Nation'—Propaganda as History." *Massachusetts Review* 20 (autumn 1979).

"Mirror for Americans: A Century of Reconstruction History." Presidential address delivered at the annual meeting of the American Historical Association, New York, December 28, 1979. *American Historical Review* 85 (February 1980).

"American Indians, Blacks, Chicanos, and Puerto Ricans." *Daedalus: Journal of the American Academy of Arts and Sciences* (1981).

"The Land of Room Enough." *Daedalus: Journal of the American Academy of Arts and Sciences* 110 (spring 1981).

"Education and National Responsibility." The John Hamilton Fulton Memorial Lecture in the Liberal Arts, Middlebury College, Middlebury, Vermont, September 22, 1981.

"George Washington Williams: The Massachusetts Years." Proceedings of the American Antiquarian Society 92 (October 1982).

"On Thinking about History." *How To Think Straight Series,* Duke University (March 1984).

"A Modest Achievement" [The Civil Rights Act of 1964]. *Focus* (October 1984).

"A Continuing Climate of Racism." *Duke Magazine* (November/December 1984).

"The Use and Misuse of the Lincoln Legacy." *Papers of the Abraham Lincoln Association,* Springfield, Illinois, 7 (1985). Reprinted in *Illinois History* (February 1990).

"Lincoln's Evolving View of Freedom." *Brown Alumni Monthly* (February 1985). Reprinted in *Books at Brown* 31–32 (1984–1985); *Sino-American Relations* 17 (winter 1991).

"The Forerunners." *American Visions* (January/February 1986).

"Southern History: The Black-White Connection." *Atlanta Historical Journal* (summer 1986).

"The Foundations: From Whom All Blessings Flow." *Scholarship Today: The Humanities and Social Sciences.* Washington, D.C.: Library of Congress, 1987.

"The Desperate Need for Black Teachers: A Special Appeal from John Hope Franklin." *Change* 14 (May/June 1987). Reprinted in *Education Digest* (March 1988).

"A Life of Learning." The Charles Homer Haskins Lecture, American Council of Learned Societies, New York, 1988.

"Opening the Door of Opportunity." *Journal of the National Medical Association* 80 (1988).

"As We Were Saying: A Historian of the United States in the People's Republic of China." *American Studies International* 26 (April 1988).

"Washington's Shameful History of Racial Bigotry." *Washington Post,* April 17, 1988.

"Afro-American History: State of the Art." *Journal of American History* 75 (June 1988).

"Race and the Constitution in the Nineteenth Century." *Update,* American Bar Association (fall 1988).

"Quasi-Free." *Stanford Lawyer* (spring/summer 1989).

"What Europeans Should Understand about African-American History." Ernst Fraenkel Lecture, Kennedy Institute for North-American Studies, Free University of Berlin, 1990.

"The Civil Rights Act of 1866 Revisited." Matthew O. Tobriner Lecture, *Hastings Law Journal* (July 1990).

"W. E. B. Du Bois: A Personal Memoir." *Massachusetts Review* 31 (autumn 1990).

"Their War and Mine." A Round Table: The Living and Reliving of World War II. *Journal of American History* 77 (September 1990).

"Who Divided This House?" *Chicago History* (fall/winter 1990–1991).

"Runaway Slaves: Counting the Cost." *American Visions* (February 1991).

"Traversing the Road to Race and History." *Forum* (spring 1991).

"The Emancipation Proclamation: An Act of Justice." *Prologue, Quarterly of the National Archives and Records Administration* (summer 1993).

V. RECORDINGS

"First-Person Singular." PBS, 1998.

"Tutu and Franklin: A Journey Towards Peace." Douglas Spiro, Renee Poussaint, and others. Washington, D.C.: Wisdom Works, 2001. VHS Tape.

VI. GENERAL EDITORSHIP

American History Series, with A. S. Eisenstadt. Wheeling, Ill.: Harlan Davidson, 1968– .

University of Chicago Press Series on Negro American Biographies and Autobiographies, 1969– .

About the Contributors

MARY FRANCES BERRY is the Geraldine R. Segal Professor of History at the University of Pennsylvania and Chairperson of the United States Commission on Civil Rights.

JOHN W. FRANKLIN is Program Manager and Curator at the Smithsonian Institution's Center for Folklife and Cultural Heritage. He began presenting Culture of Africa and Its Diaspora at the Smithsonian Folklife Festival in 1976 while living and teaching in Dakar, Senegal. From 1987 to 1992, Franklin planned symposia and seminars for the Smithsonian's Office of Interdisciplinary Studies before joining the Center for Folklife, where he has curated a number of programs.

GEORGE M. FREDRICKSON is Professor Emeritus from the Department of History at Stanford University. He is the author of numerous books, including *The Black Image in the White Mind: The Debate on Afro-American Character and Destiny, 1817–1914* and *Racism: A Short History.*

ROBERT L. HARRIS, JR., is Vice Provost for Diversity and Faculty Development at Cornell University, where he is also Associate Professor of African American History in the Africana Studies and Research Center. He is the author of *Teaching African American History,* published by the American Historical Association.

WALTER B. HILL, JR., is Senior Archivist and the Subject Area Specialist for African American History and Federal Records at the National Archives and Records Administration. He is also Adjunct Professor of Afro-American Studies at Howard University.

DARLENE CLARK HINE is John A. Hannah Professor of History at Michigan State University in East Lansing. She is coeditor with Jacqueline McLeod of *Crossing Boundaries: Comparative History of Black People in Diaspora;* coauthor with Kathleen Thompson of *A Shining Thread of Hope: The History of Black Women in America* and with William C. Hine and Stanley Harrold of *The African American Odyssey;* and author of a new edition of *Black Victory: The Rise and Fall of the White Primary in Texas.* Hine was President of the Organization of American Historians (2001–2002) and President of the Southern Historical Association (2002–2003).

BEVERLY JARRETT is Director and Editor-in-Chief of the University of Missouri Press. She has known John Hope Franklin for nearly thirty of her forty years in the publishing business and has been privileged to work with him on a number of his books.

SUSAN KING received her M.A. in history from Virginia Commonwealth University in Richmond, Virginia. She is the Editorial Assistant at the University of Missouri Press.

DAVID LEVERING LEWIS is University Professor and Professor of History at New York University. He has written books on African American, European, and African history. His two-volume biography of W. E. B. Du Bois won the Pulitzer Prize for biography in 1994 and 2001, as well as the Bancroft and Parkman prizes in 1994.

GENNA RAE MCNEIL is Professor of History at the University of North Carolina–Chapel Hill. She is the author of *Groundwork: Charles Hamilton Houston and the Struggle for Civil Rights* and coeditor of several books, including *African Americans and Jews in the Twentieth Century: Studies in Convergence and Conflict* and, with John Hope Franklin, *African Americans and the Living Constitution.*

ALFRED A. MOSS, JR., is Associate Professor of History at the University of Maryland in College Park and an Episcopal priest. In addition to serving as a coauthor of the sixth, seventh, and eighth editions of *From Slavery to Freedom: A History of African Americans,* he is the author of *The American Negro Academy: Voice of the Talented Tenth* and coauthor of *Looking at History* and *Dangerous Donations: Northern Philanthropy and Southern Black Education, 1902–1930.*

LOREN SCHWENINGER is the Elizabeth Rosenthal Excellence Professor at the University of North Carolina at Greensboro. The author or editor of five books on African American history, including *Black Property Owners in the South, 1790–1915,* he is currently the director of the Race and Slavery Petitions Project.

DARYL MICHAEL SCOTT is professor of history at Howard University. He is the author of *Contempt and Pity: Social Policy and the Image of the Damaged Black Psyche, 1880–1996,* which won the 1998 James Rawley Prize of the Organization of American Historians. He is currently working on *The Lost World of White Nationalism: White Self-Rule in the American South, 1865–1965.*